EXPLORATION IN TEXAS
ANCIENT & OTHERWISE

John L. Davis

Exploration in Texas
Ancient & Otherwise
  With Thoughts on the Nature of Evidence
by John L. Davis

Copyright 1984
The University of Texas
  Institute of Texan Cultures at San Antonio
Jack R. Maguire, Executive Director

Designer and Typesetter: Meredith Rees
Editor: Sandra Hodsdon Carr

Library of Congress Catalog Card Number 84-80759
International Standard Book Numbers
  Hardbound 086701-018-5
  Softbound 086701-019-3

This publication was made possible, in part, by a grant from
The Houston Endowment, Inc.

Printed in the United States of America

EXPLORATION IN TEXAS
ANCIENT & OTHERWISE
WITH THOUGHTS ON
THE NATURE OF EVIDENCE

JOHN L. DAVIS

The University of Texas
Institute of Texan Cultures at San Antonio
1984

INTRODUCTION

This is an unusual book, but then Dr. John L. Davis is an unusual writer.

As both a dedicated scholar and a prolific author, his previous books have explored such diverse subjects as the Texas Rangers, Spanish shipwrecks, and the histories of Houston and San Antonio. In other peripatetic forays he has produced a volume attesting the thesis that Texas had a role in the American Revolution of 1776, a work on the supposed humor of William Blake, and papers on the history and occurrence of vampirism.

In this latest result of his serious research, however, he looks far beyond recorded — at least, beyond provable — history and suggests that explorers from far lands may have traveled Texas thirty-six centuries ago. Could it be that a Chinese was the first non-native to discover America?

The reader is left to draw his own conclusions; Dr. Davis presents only the evidence as he has found it. And the story he has turned up is fascinating indeed.

In these pages one sails with the Africans, Phoenicians, and Carthaginians across an unknown Atlantic; sees Columbus and his sailors disagree as to where they actually stopped in 1492, and learns of a strange tablet found in the Big Bend of Texas which may, or may not, be evidence that Mediterranean people reached the area centuries before the accepted discovery of the New World.

It is like a good mystery story in which all known facts are presented, but the solution is left to the reader. Or there is no solution. . . . The book is not, finally, about the earlier explorers, but about the nature of fact and evidence.

This is high adventure, expertly told by a scholar who also can write. It is a book to be savored, then studied, and then read again and again.

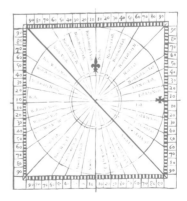

Jack Maguire
Executive Director
The Institute of Texan Cultures

FOREWORD

"Who were the first people to explore this place?" is one of the most commonly asked questions anywhere. Curiosity itself may lead to speculation, and questions of historical "firsts" seem to attract wild stories, guesses, or questionable documents as well as to generate abundant historical teeth-gnashing. A few people have spent lifetimes and wagered reputations digging for and presenting the facts. But what are the facts? What are facts?

Most stories claiming "first arrivals" are hard to prove. Proof of the stories is not the object of this book. Many of the stories mentioned here are not accepted as fact, or as proven, by the majority of scholars. Yet, happily, facts are not the only end product of a search.

This book speaks of three things. First, it collects some of the more controversial stories of Old World explorers who may have come to the Texas area before A.D. 1520—but not including the American Indians. They may be regarded as settlers or immigrants or natives—not explorers.

The second topic concerns the nature of an explorer: what he does and how he is different from other people such as settlers or immigrants.

The third and main topic concerns the nature of facts and proof, truth and evidence. What are they? Just what is a fact in the humanities? If something is speculative, what good is it? These are important considerations not only in the context of early explorers but also in everyday life.

ACKNOWLEDGMENTS

The main acknowledgments, and thanks, go to the initial readers who slogged through an early draft, pointing out errors and corrections that should be made in fact and tone: Dr. Thomas R. Hester, Dora Guerra, Dr. Jeremiah F. Epstein, Dr. Tom Gibbons, Dr. Roger Bailey, Anders Saustrup, Rosemary Catacalos, Dr. William Newcomb, David Haynes, and Rosemary Davis. They are responsible for helping with large matters from arguments over epistemology to Chinese translation, tone of language to references. The correspondents are too numerous to mention here, but they were important to many a concern. Remaining errors of fact and interpretation are, I hope, entirely my own.

Special thanks go to Pete Graeber and Nella Tolk for having me aboard the cutter *Defiance* where I learned a bit about sailing—and thereupon collected experiences which were useful in judging assorted data surfacing in later days and nights.

NOTE ON THE NOTES

The notes in this book, I hope it is not really necessary to point out, are themselves a display, or exhibit, in Pound's words, of examples of evidence. They are so in most books. Here, the reader should consider which are enlightening or confusing, which seem to be necessary or unnecessary, which are defensive, pompous, useful, and so on, realizing that the standards for such judgment are in the reader's head and that the standards are the subject of this book.

The notes are keyed to the general bibliography by the author's name and, where necessary, by the first words of the title.

The not-so-helpful reference term *passim* is used only where numerous page references would have had to be cited *and* the topic is readily traceable in the source index *or* the reference is quite generally concerned with a broad topic, e.g. Chinese history. However tempting, *passim* is not here intended as equivalent to "I've forgotten the specific reference" or "read the whole thing like I had to."

j.l.d.

CONTENTS

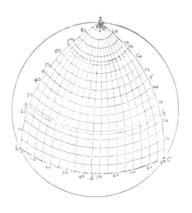

SOME CHINESE STORIES: THE OTHER "FAR EAST"

A group of explorers paused in the brilliant afternoon. They looked out over the last few yards of sand and gravel to a river that boiled around rocks as it emerged from the canyon. In places dark green cane grew almost down to the brown water. The tall, jagged sides of a mountain were etched in the sunlight above them.

One of the men shaded his eyes and pondered a piece of blue-green rock he had picked up. Behind the travelers were a hundred miles of land covered by cactus and yucca, with grasses and trees growing along intermittent streams.

The man standing in front walked down to the river, dropped his pack, pushed back his hat, and sat down on a rock. His few companions did likewise, taking off their sandals and bathing their feet in the turbulent water where it ran up on the sand, cold in the sunshine.

From his pack the man took a notebook, which was made of a few strips of local cane, dried and shaved almost flat, laced together with a cord at one end. Earlier he had written on thin pieces of wood, but his supply of these had run out. Taking a small square stone from his pack, he dipped a bit of water into its low depression. He then started rubbing a stick of solid ink into the water. Gradually the water turned black. Setting the freshly-made ink to one side, he took a small brush between his

fingers, then looked around at the clear day for a moment before beginning to write.

"Have walked about three hundred li since Bald Mountain. Here, Bamboo Mountain is near the river which looks like a boundary. There is no grass, or trees, but some jasper and jade stones. The river is impeded in its course here by rocks, but flows on southeast to the great body of water. . . ."

Santa Elena Canyon, the Big Bend

[1] Or Shan-hai-king (Leland) or Shan Hai Ching (Shao), etc. A transliteration of 山海經 is, like all such, probably impossible. The forms used in this book, although they reproduce inconsistencies even in the use of the hyphen, reflect the most common, older forms used in the indexes of the major references . . . most commonly the Wade-Giles system. But times are changing. Peking is already Beijing; Fa Hsien becomes Faxian; Shan Hai King becomes Shanhai Jing; but Fusang seems to be remaining Fusang (see Fang Zhongpu or Luo Rongqu).

Years later the account this man was writing would find its way into one of the oldest books in the world, the Shan Hai King,[1] often called the Mountain-Sea Classic or the Classic of Mountains and Seas. Edited at least three times and subjected to one national bookburning, it survived and retained the story of explorations over unknown lands.

The man was Chinese, the time was perhaps 3,600 years ago, and he had been walking across part of what was later called the trans-Pecos area of Texas.

And that statement and the foregoing scene are speculative—Yet perhaps not entirely fictional. This is one of the best examples of a historical account that *could* be true.[2] The story is just tantalizing enough to be fascinating, and this interpretation of it is speculative enough to drive many historians into a frenzy.

To be able to judge the truth of the story—to consider the evidence for the story—a person needs to know a few elements of Chinese history, beginning with a look at the Shan Hai King. This book, containing a wide variety of accounts and stories, often is called the world's oldest geography.[3] It is also one of the earliest works of Chinese literature. In addition to geographical descriptions, it speaks of monsters and weird beasts, myths and wild tales; and it includes enough of these to cause many scholars either to brand the work nonsense or to ignore it completely.[4]

However, it contains no more wonders than other records which are accepted as generally true by later critical readers. Many European works regarded as classics are laced with metaphor (or outright lies), but these entire works are not therefore condemned.[5] Sir Walter Raleigh speaks of headless warriors; Marco Polo writes of the Orc, a bird so big it could fly off with an elephant in its talons; Herodotus, one of the greatest Greek historians, includes winged serpents and ants as large as oxen; and even the level-headed conqueror Julius Caesar, in his account of northwestern Europe, speaks of the unicorn and of elk which never lie down to rest. Yet the basic reliability of these writers is not questioned.

But even if an occasional monster can be overlooked, there are other problems. The date of the Shan Hai King is hard to estimate. Furthermore, no certain author is known. Such things worry scholars. Early Chinese writers ascribed the work to Yu, Minister of Public Works under Emperor Shun, in 2205 B.C.[6] The date is regarded by most historians as being too early—much too early—in the near-legendary Hsia Dynasty.[7] Yet, since the turn of the present century, archaeologists in China have steadily pushed back the dates of known cultural achievements.[8] Dynasties mentioned in earlier classics, once considered legend, have been documented through recent field work. It appears more and more likely that China's civilization has all the antiquity ascribed to it by its oldest stories. But there are still other problems with accepting the document.

Could the Chinese have carried out such a journey some forty centuries ago?

For generations historians considered that the Chinese were not an ocean-going people. This opinion has largely changed.[9] The Chinese are now known to have sailed open-ocean vessels since the eleventh century B.C. and probably earlier. Stone anchors, of the style carried by early Chinese vessels, have been found off the California coast, but their authenticity is in doubt.[10] Absolute proof, such as remains of Chinese ocean-going ships, cannot be dated to the time of the Shan Hai King, but descriptions of Chinese ships of a somewhat later time indicate previous ship development.

[2] See the general Chinese references, note 11; for climate, see McGregor, Jannings, Wendorf, Bryant, Schoenwetter, and Flint; for methods of writing, see Loewe, "Wooden and Bamboo Strips," 13, and Young, 27. Ink sticks, brushes, even the strip notebooks *may* be anachronistic. Scholars do not agree. The National Palace Museum dates ink and brushes before 1100 B.C. Western references (Lowe, for example) say brushes do not date before 201 B.C.

[3] Vining, 669 (quoting de Rosny from *La Civilisation Japonaise*, Paris, 1883).

[4] Vining, 643, 669. See also note 9.

[5] Vining, 451-52 for a discussion of other "errors" in European accounts.

[6] If one accepts the list of earlier rulers. See the comments of M. Bazin Sr., in an article from the *Journal Asiatique* reprinted in Vining, 670f, which summarizes earlier accounts.

[7] Leland, 12.

[8] Chang, *passim;* Creel, *passim.*

[9] See Fang Zhongpu citing his own opinions and those of Jia Lanpo and Frost.

[10] Fang Zhongpu, 66, believes in their authenticity. For the other side of the story, see the excellent examinations by Frost and Luo Rongqu.

A Chinese warship, c. 1520

[11] General statements on Chinese history are based on Ho, Chang, Needham, Watson, Li, Creel, Hopkins, and Breuer. See Chang, *Shang Civilization,* particularly for dating.

The Shang Dynasty, the earliest so far confirmed by most modern archaeological studies, existed from the eighteenth to the thirteenth centuries B.C. and was an advanced culture.[11] The Chinese of this period were highly learned: they had a written language; a bronze fabricating technology; fully developed institutions such as art, agriculture, and government; distinctive architecture, plumbing, weapons, musical instruments, chariots, and all the items that archaeologists call material culture. They also had practices that are not socially acceptable today, such as human sacrifice. Yet it seems clear that had they wanted to, Shang people could have put a party of explorers on another continent.

But did they?

That question causes one to look closely at the evidence of the Shan Hai King. It is a written record but a curiously choppy account which reads like a collection of notes.

The book in existence today is not the complete, original record. Even though the Chinese people are very devoted to their classics and are constant note-takers and compilers of encyclopaedias, they have at various times in their history allowed written records to lapse. In 213 B.C. the emperor Ch'in Shih Huang decided to abolish all records of the past. He was not the first, nor the last, dictator to decide that accurate knowledge of the past was a dangerous thing in the minds and hands of the people. His premier, Li Ssu, suggested that destroying books—selected books, to be sure—would accomplish the desire to control information rather neatly. The effort was made but was ultimately unsuccessful. Books hidden in walls and wells later came to light.

By the fifth century A.D. the volume of records and books in China had grown to such a total that no one could hope to read even a small fraction of those in existence. This was a different problem. The government decreed a massive editing project during which almost all former written works were read by teams of scholars and condensed. The originals were destroyed.

In the thirteenth century more condensation was ordered, and even the fifth century versions were cut down. Again, the "originals" were discarded. The enormous effort was understandable. One encyclopaedia, in manuscript form, had grown to the equivalent length of 22,937 books.

Because of such condensation and destruction, the Shan Hai King, originally about thirty-two books long, also exists in an eighteen-book version, each book from one to thirty pages in length and most in summary form.[12] Thus, more than one version exists. What is reprinted today is most certainly not the whole story.

Here is some of what is left:

. . . to the south, Lone Mountain is found. Upon this there are many gems and much gold, and below it many beautiful stones. Muddy River is found here, a stream flowing southeasterly into a mighty flood, in which there are many T'iao-Yung. These look like yellow serpents with fish's fins. . . .

And it says that, three hundred li to the south, Bald Mountain is found . . . wild animals are found here which look like suckling pigs, but they have pearls. They are called Tung-Tung, their name being given to them in imitation of their cry. The Hwan River is found here, a stream flowing easterly into a river . . . one authority says that it flows into the sea. In this there are many water-gems [quartz or agate crystals].

. . . three hundred li to the south, Bamboo Mountain is found, bordering on a river. One authority says that it is on the shore — or that it is at the boundary line. There is no grass, or trees, but there are many green-jasper and green-jade stones. The Kih River [water impeded in its course by rocks] is found here, a stream flowing into T'su-Tan River [or body of water]. In this [country] there is a great abundance of dye plants.[13]

[12] Vining, 669, discusses this (quoting from the *Catalogue des Livres Chinois,* Paris, 1873).

[13] See Appendix 1 for text; the li is perhaps about ⅓ mile, 486 yards (Quatrefages, 203).

These are the descriptions of some of the last sections of a land traverse that covers a dozen points of geographical interest along a generally north-south line. The Shan Hai King records three such traverses in this section and two others in subsequent books. Although the hand of an editor is obvious, it sounds neither whimsical nor mythical. The notes are not complete (or they suffered in the condensations), but they do give distances between major mountains and drainage patterns and some notes on plants and animals. The accounts do appear to be an explorer's record of a new land.

The first question later readers had was where this land might be. There is enough description left to confirm distances between prominent mountain peaks, observe the proper direction rivers flow, and match the occurrence of some minerals, animals, and plants.

Many generations of scholars searched for routes in China or other parts of Asia which would fit the descriptions. Matching land forms were not found there.[14] The Shan Hai King notes that the traverses are in a place beyond the eastern sea from China—and the routes do match mountains and rivers in parts of Canada, the western United States, Texas, and Mexico. In the section quoted above, the course appears to be along part of a line of peaks through Wyoming, Colorado, New Mexico, and Texas. Mountain peaks, wooded and desert areas, stretches of sand, and river directions fit the description.

Lone Mountain may be Guadalupe Peak, highest mountain in Texas near the Texas-New Mexico border, and very much a lone peak, with Delaware Creek draining east into the Pecos. About a hundred miles (three hundred li) south is Mount Livermore, or Baldy, as it is called even today,[15] and the animals here are surely peccary, with pearl-like tusks. Limpia Creek,

[14] Vining, 670f; Mertz, *passim.*

[15] The translation of T'ai as "bald" is questionable. The translation used here is largely that of Vining with help from Dr. Roger Bailey, San Antonio College, San Antonio. Vining's citation is Williams's dictionary, which does not give "bald" as a translation, but does give "slippery" and "smooth" as possible readings. The character can also be read as "large" or "extensive" (Wieger, 643). The etymology of the character T'ai seems to be water held inside of both hands with "great" added. This would be slippery indeed. Some rocks in the Davis Mountains area are very slippery after a sudden rain, but this seems to be going too far afield. Perhaps

Guadalupe Peak and El Capitan

although hardly a river now, flows east. And there are enough beautiful "water gems"—agate and quartz—in the area to satisfy the description.

There are two possible routes south. About a hundred miles south and east is the Emory Peak area, part of the Big Bend, with a logical route down Terlingua Creek to the west. The Rio Grande, indeed impeded there, breaks out of the spectacular Santa Elena Canyon. Or, the explorers, going less than a hundred miles, may have swung to the west, ending up at the river after skirting the Chinati Mountains.[16] Along either route, a local dye plant in great abundance is the creosote bush.

The three quoted sections would hardly be called good evidence. Three locations, taken alone and only generally describing the landscape, would prove nothing. But the whole traverse from Wyoming to Texas—correctly mentioning rivers, desert areas, wildlife, distance between notable mountains, minerals, and plants—is more convincing. And comparisons of the Chinese text with maps and field observations show that five routes in the Shan Hai King fit more or less accurately on land in the western part of North America.[17] This would seem to be more than coincidence. At least the routes do not fit China, and there is nowhere else to put them (South America was even tried, with no success).[18]

it is best to stay with Vining's interpretation that the intended meaning is a smooth, bare, slippery mountain, analogic to "bald" as used geographically. See Williams's dictionary, 848, 991, 962, lxxiv, and lxxi (the 1874 edition).

[16] Author's field work; Johnson and Maxwell, *passim;* Mertz, *passim.*

[17] Mertz, *passim;* U.S. Army maps; author's field work.

[18] Mertz, 112.

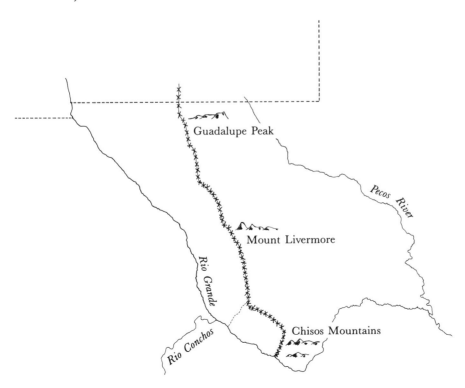

But such evidence satisfies few people—and for good reasons. Unlike the conquests of Caesar in Europe, there is almost no other evidence the Chinese were here. For a statement to be considered "unquestionably" true, there usually has to be supporting evidence of several kinds.

A few things have been noticed: American Indian legends mention the arrival of strangers long before Europeans;[19] certain prehistoric earth mounds in Mississippi are similar to some in China;[20] particular stone axes and blades are much the same—indeed, one Chinese story relates how stone points were offered the emperor Yu as souvenirs.[21] North American Indian and Shang artists alike depict animal forms as if the body were split with joined halves.[22] Central American legends speak of the gifts of language and agriculture being brought by travelers.[23] One cache of old Chinese coins was found by miners in British Columbia in 1882, but not under conditions that would guarantee it had been hidden at a pre-Columbian date.[24] This kind of data, however, can easily be coincidence or hoax.[25] Final decisions cannot be made on the basis of such things.[26]

Even a number of other documents telling the same story would add support, but no other records speaking of such a journey at this early date have yet been found.

Interestingly, one other Chinese document does seem to describe a much later visit to North America—some twenty-two centuries later. It is an account told by a Buddhist priest, on his arrival at a Chinese court about A.D. 500 from what he considered to be the far east. His name was Hwui Shan,[27] and he should be heard next.

> Fu Sang is twenty thousand li or more to the east of the Great Han country, which is east of the Middle Kingdom [China]. The region has many Fu Sang trees, giving the country its name. The leaves of the Fu Sang resemble T'ung and the first sprouts are like bamboo. The people of the country eat them and a fruit which is like a pear, but red in color.
>
> They spin thread from the bark [of the Fu Sang] from which they make cloth. They make houses of planks, but have no walled cities. They have a written language and use the bark of the Fu Sang to make paper. . . .

Hwui Shan commented at length on the system of justice, the method a ruler follows in assuming power, the colors and style of the ruler's clothing, ceremonial processions, social ranks in the land, and the presence of cattle (perhaps bison) and deer.

[19] Mackenzie, *passim.*

[20] Vining, 193. On mounds, see Silverberg, *passim.* The mounds have been attributed to everyone, including pre-Christian Danes who wandered south to become Toltecs (Barton as quoted in Silverberg, 30f).

[21] Creel, 46, discusses origin of blades in China; Krieger as quoted by Mertz, 99.

[22] Li, 31.

[23] Mackenzie, *passim.*

[24] Vining, 184.

[25] Epstein, *passim,* on the nature of evidence not only concerning coins but also the conditions under which coins are lost.

[26] Note how the stories creep into the contemporary press, e.g. Noorbergen. See also Riley, sec. 15: 293, on "Pre-Columbian Contacts."

[27] Or Hui Shen, Huishen, etc., see note 1. His monastic name may have been Huiji (Fang Zhongpu, 65).

"The ground is destitute of iron, but it has copper. They do not value gold and silver and have no taxes in the markets."[28] The priest went on to outline wedding customs and the manner of burial. He also noted carefully that the people of the land were ignorant of the Buddha's way of life until about A.D. 458 when the five priests voyaged to that country and tried to convert them.

[28] The Liang-shu, see Hwui Shan and Vining, bibliography.

Reconstructed drawing of a Chinese court, c. 831

Added to the priest's account in the court record is a story of certain unnamed men who a few years later (A.D. 507) were crossing the sea and were blown ashore in the unknown land. Their story confirms some of the priest's comments. The women of the country to the far east resembled Chinese women, but their language could not be understood. The men had human bodies, but dog heads and dog voices. These people made round adobe houses, the doors of which resembled burrows.

It sounds like a wild story, but to judge the account, one must consider the history of the document, the existence of the priest himself, and another slice of Chinese history. How the priest's story was written is particularly important because it explains why some of the descriptions of the land and peoples far to the east are hard to understand or to believe.

The story of Hwui Shan was recorded in the Liang-shu, the Records of the Liang Dynasty, a part of the Nan-shih,

29 The text speaks also of Hwui Shan as being from Fu Sang, but this reference does not imply he was a native of the New World.

or History of the South, written by Li Yen-shau who lived in the seventh century. The account was copied by Ma Twan-lin in his "Antiquarian Researches," published in 1321. Both versions are copies of the earlier court records.

No one now knows Hwui Shan's homeland.[29] It may have been perhaps within present-day Afghanistan or Kashmir. He almost certainly had only crossed China, or had been there only for a short time, before his long journey. His name is simply an epithet meaning "very intelligent," similar to names taken by many another priest.

The priest apparently made a successful return from a most interesting and almost unknown land far to the east, but he had trouble telling his story. China was in disarray.

Around A.D. 500 China was embroiled in civil wars and split into northern and southern kingdoms. Ruling families and capital cities shifted like autumn leaves. Hwui Shan bided his time.

In A.D. 502 the Southern Ch'i Dynasty, with Chien-k'ang (Nanking) as its capital, was overthrown by Liang Wu Ti. He established the Liang Dynasty which for a short time was stable. It suddenly became possible for Hwui Shan to appear at court.

The choice of the southern capital for a reception was a good one, both for the priest and for the record which exists today. Emperor Wu Ti was not only a good ruler by the standards of the day but also a patron of Buddhism. Hwui Shan, who probably could speak little court Chinese, was nevertheless heard politely, and it was realized that his story was a most unusual one. In fifth-century China a land far to the east was known only as a myth—a land where the sun was born and used as subject matter only by poets. But what the priest said rang true—or the court was just being polite.

When the priest related his story, a number of noble-men were at court. One of them, Yu-kie, was asked by the emperor to question Hwui Shan further, translate, and write his story for the court records. Working together, certainly misunderstanding each other from time to time, Hwui Shan and Yu-kie produced a short narrative of the journey.[30] But the Chinese court of the day was, if anything, highly cultured, and Yu-kie could not resist writing a parallel version of his own, satiric and interspersed with humorous comments.

30 Vining, 448, for a further discussion.

Literary scholars rather enjoy these two versions of the land of Fu Sang; historians, however, are a bit uneasy with the second version because a humorous document is always an uncertain record. How can one decide when the author is being serious?

But the versions are identifiable. Hwui Shan's is matter-of-fact for the most part. Yu-kie's version has the thread of Hwui Shan's words, but the bulk of it is humorous burlesque on a basic story. They support one another, however, and give a check on the basic facts.

The story is that Hwui Shan and his companions traveled east from China about thirteen thousand miles and, from a coast, traveled inland at least three hundred fifty miles. They met many primitive people along the way and, once in the far eastern land, saw other people who had heads of dogs and lived in round adobe homes. Traveling on, they reached a relatively civilized people having a written language, a type of paper, a government, buildings, and a culture perhaps like that of Indians of central Mexico. Hwui Shan described the geography only generally but had much to say of the social organization of the people.

It is not known what the emperor thought of the priest's story, but into the court records it went. More than a thousand years passed before anyone else apparently wondered where Hwui Shan might have been.

Western scholars made the first controversial comments about the story. In 1753 Phillippe Buache made the outrageous suggestion that Buddhist priests had established a colony on the west coast of America.[31] In 1761 Joseph de Guignes presented a paper to the French Royal Academy concerning Hwui Shan's account. Not only did he give a translation of the priest's words, but also de Guignes maintained that Fu Sang was Mexico and that the final people described by Hwui Shan were the Indians of Mexico and the southwestern United States. For some years there was a curious scholarly silence. Then in 1831 Julius Klaproth, an eminent German scholar, attacked de Guignes's view, and the fight was on. The contention quickly attracted a handful of other scholars. Even to this day the argument has not been resolved.[32]

The first disputes were personally bitter and poetically violent, in the style of academic contention that was to endure until the early 1900's. Since those original arguments, a few others have analyzed the account, argued over it, and tried to prove — or disprove — that the land of Fu Sang was Mexico or the southwestern United States. Some of the priest's story fits. The men with dog heads could be Pueblo Indians. Such masks are still worn. Certainly the Indians look somewhat Chinese, although their language is different, as the priest noted.

The multi-use Fu Sang plant — source of fiber, thread, food, and drink — is possibly the maguey, the century plant. The red, pear-shaped fruit could be either early American corn, such

[31] Shao, 6.

[32] Vining, *passim*, for the best summary; supporters are Leland and Mertz; examples of opponents of writers like Mertz are Shao and Wauchope (102, especially); Henning, 34-41.

The Chisos Mountains in the Big Bend, c. 1937

as has been found in abandoned storage pits, or the tuna of the nopal — the fruit of the prickly pear cactus — still a common food.

The circular houses were common in the Mogollon culture of the southwestern United States around A.D. 350 and later.[33] The social customs match fairly well — or can be made to match — much that is known about the pre-Aztec Indians of central Mexico and the southwestern Indians of California, Arizona, New Mexico, and Texas.

The journey itself — via the Aleutian current or along the coast — is a plausible one.[34] It is even possible for unmanned ships to drift to the California coast, as evidenced by many a Japanese wreck, particularly in the favorable autumn winds.[35]

What the priest describes along the way also matches the culture of some former Siberian and Alaskan peoples, as far as they are known today. And the geographical sites he mentions, including descriptions of places hard to miss such as the La Brea tar pits of California, seem to fit.

Even the stranger comments — a kingdom of women, ladies taking serpents for husbands, and men speaking with the voices of dogs — can be explained, if one grants the changes that the Chinese text must have gone through. Hopi tradition, for example, was largely matriarchal and the ladies there did wed serpents — members of the Snake Clan who considered themselves physically one with snakes. Hwui Shan would have had a hard

[33] McGregor, *passim.*

[34] For a compilation, though not to the Americas, see Mills (particularly his preface-bibliography, 3-4); Chapman, 21-30. For an earlier, general reference to the area, see Coxe.

[35] Bancroft, vol. V, 51-53; Beazley, 502; Davies, 112.

time trying to explain that to Yu-kie. In addition, the Chinese were very fond of offering insults and half-insults to the language and the physical aspects of foreigners. Language that sounded like the barking of dogs or men who looked like filthy devils are common epithets in some Chinese texts for even close neighbors.[36]

But again, the only evidence of the priest's journey is an old document mentioning similarities which very well might just be coincidence.

Since the days of the start of the controversy—but rarely outside professional papers—various authors have devoted themselves to establishing cultural links between pre-Spanish Mexico and the Orient. Similarities have been noted in art, religion, myth, architecture, and social institutions. It is said of some Mexican antiquities that had they not been found in the Americas, they would have been called colonial Chinese without question.[37] Some Chinese and Japanese images of the Buddha are so similar to Mexican jades that they could be interchanged; some carved wall designs are similar; the earlier Spanish explorers in the west reported seeing strange trading ships;[38] there are resemblances in the calendars, and one of the oldest New World pottery styles is virtually identical to early Japanese.[39]

Indeed, the appearance of the bow and arrow can be dated about A.D. 500 among native American peoples of the southwest—about the time such a weapon could have been brought by Hwui Shan and his group. This statement is regarded with a wide variety of responses by archaeologists. Some think it a possibility; others consider such an idea stupid and irresponsible. Such is the variation in opinion today.

Some scholars have viewed the similarities with cautions that the fact of similarity does not mean contact between peoples. Those who want to see similarities can see them; those who do not, do not. Others can cite significant differences or claim parallel but independent development of cultural traits.[40] Even contact between peoples would not necessarily mean a colonial venture but perhaps only an exploration.[41] At the present state of archaeological knowledge, however, there are those who say that evidence in support of early cultural connections across the Pacific Ocean appears to be better than the evidence that there were cultural relations between the early peoples of the central valley of Mexico and Guatamala.[42]

A reader of such stories might also question whether a Buddhist priest of the fifth century would have had a motive for such a journey. Few Chinese perhaps had a motive, or the inclination, but for the priest the answer is almost certainly yes.[43] It

[36] Vining, 81.

[37] Heine-Geldern, "The Problem of Transpacific Influences," 278; see also Waters, 116; Mackenzie and Shao, *passim*.

[38] Gomara, saying that ships laden with merchandise—and strange to the Spanish—were seen off California (Quatrefages, 205).

[39] Meggers, "Early Formative Period," *passim*; Lommel, 74, 137.

[40] Shao, *passim*.

[41] Heine-Geldern, "The Problem of Transpacific Influence," 293, and Shao, *passim*.

[42] Meggers, *Prehistoric America*, 66f.

[43] Beazley, 468; Shao, 10.

[44] Giles, introduction; Leowe, "Spices and Silk," *passim,* for other aspects of trade.

[45] Kennedy, 219f.

[46] Beazley, 475f.

[47] Beazley, 472; Needham, sec. 7, "Travel of Ideas and Techniques," 176-80, 206-11, 223-25.

[48] Giles, *passim;* Beazley, 479; Legge, *passim.*

[49] Beazley, 486.

is particularly believable that Buddhist priests would have made such a trip.[44]

Traveling Buddhist priests and scholars, such as the famous Fa-Hsien, traveled west, south, and north over all of Asia and most of Africa and Europe as pilgrims and missionaries of the first major religion to actively take its belief to others.[45] Buddhist priests were particularly active in the fifth and sixth centuries.[46] They apparently even visited early Britain and the Roman Empire, often leaving written records that are not questioned—as long as the journey does not cross the Pacific Ocean.[47]

Fa-Hsien, Buddhist traveler of the fifth century, journeyed from China across central Asia, came back into India from the west, took ship for Ceylon, traveled across the Indian Ocean, around Sumatra, across the China Sea and back home. It was a stupendous journey, and his written accounts sound much like Hwui Shan's.[48] This journey is believed in spite of his notes about "evil spirits," Buddha's shadow left on a rock, and an invisible, white-eared dragon. Like Hwui Shan's account, his journey is also a human story of hardship and faith. Unlike Hwui Shan's, it is accepted as true.[49]

The explorer Fa-Hsien regards a fallen companion

So the question might become—When an account of A.D. 500 is read that speaks of going the proper distance east from China to reach North America, and gives many details that could fit that strange land, why should it not be believed?[50]

[50] Larson, 109.

There are reasons. Not only is good secondary evidence lacking, but also, as far as archaeological or anthropological theory goes, many things—for some scholars—are at stake. Early contact between peoples of the Americas and the Old World is a subject highly charged with emotion today, particularly where the transmission of inventions and beliefs might be involved.[51] Even the consideration of "insignificant" contact creates great interest and argument.

[51] Meggers, *Prehistoric America*, 4-5; Gladwin, *passim.*

If it is ever proven that mankind's common inventions, art forms, or beliefs were made independently in many areas of the world, this would support the innate inventiveness and perhaps even inevitableness of mankind's achievements. It would also mean man's culture is not unique to any place in this world—or perhaps in another world. And it might mean that lost cultural accomplishments are probably regained.

If, on the other hand, major things are only invented once and thereafter passed on from person to person, the culture of man is apparently unique, even accidental—and susceptible to permanent loss. In this case, no one can count on man's culture to regenerate if destroyed.[52]

[52] The anthropological "schools" of "independent invention" and "contact" theories of cultural advance (parallel evolution and diffusion) have argued the point for generations. See Taylor, Morgan, Boas, Schmidt, and Lowie.

At present, the stories of an early Chinese explorer and a wandering Buddhist priest have no unquestionably supporting facts outside of a few old documents and cultural observations which could be coincidence. This is evidence which by no means forms what is known as "proof."

Indeed, many archaeologists today question all evidence related to the topic of Old World arrivals at any period before Columbus. In their definition American archaeology is *only* American Indian archaeology.[53]

[53] Author's experience; also see notes to chap. 2.

The most liberal opinion which attracts general support at present is that a boat or two may accidentally have been driven by storms over the Pacific in early years, but any contact was culturally insignificant.[54] In other words, no one has yet discovered the ruin of a fifth century Buddhist shrine in Texas.

[54] Davies, 103f.

But the stories remain intriguing. And they remain. They are a long way from being forgotten, and their consideration can lead to a great flexibility of thinking. That's a good thing to develop. Above all, the stories are illustrations of a basic concern: Just what is a fact? And that consideration—being able to make such a consideration—is perhaps more important than the "truth" of the stories.

WHAT IS A FACT?

Facts in the humanities—fields of concern such as history, philosophy, literary criticism—are often unlike facts in the natural sciences. They are sometimes statements about what happened or is happening ("John F. Kennedy spent the night in Fort Worth, Texas, on November 21, 1963" or "Spanish is spoken by a majority of the people in Hidalgo County"), but they are often associated with an inference or interpretation about what happened, is happening, or estimates of what will happen ("John F. Kennedy was killed the next day by a single gunman" or "Spanish will be spoken by a majority of people in Hidalgo County in the year 2100").

Now science, although it indulges in similar inference and interpretation, would like its facts ("There is no measurable difference in the speed of light measured in vacuum in different directions in the universe") to be general, always true, and reproducible on demand or at least observable in the present. Most facts in the humanities, however, cannot be tested by experiment. Often, even though specific, they cannot be directly observed.

A fact in the humanities is usually from the past, however distant or recent. It is most often a statement about a particular thing, has usually gone through several hands or heads, and is often subject to some question. Proof usually means simply that most people agree that the data, the evidence behind the fact, is reliable, correctly interpreted, and sufficient.

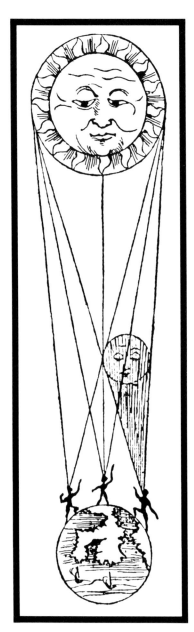

Stepping around the words "reliable," "correct," and "sufficient" for the moment, it remains that facts in the humanities are usually neither experimentally reproducible nor immediately observable. Some researchers have tried divine revelation and seances, but it apparently remains impossible now to ask Hwui Shan if he were ever in Texas or ask President Kennedy if he ever spent a night in Fort Worth. It might, however, theoretically be possible to personally ask every person in Hidalgo County if he speaks Spanish.

When one looks at records such as news stories that indicate where Kennedy was the night of November 21, 1963, one is considering secondary information (as long as Kennedy did not write the record); when one asks someone if he speaks Spanish, the reply is primary data—as would be a genuine letter written by Hwui Shan.

Primary data are often considered to be the most accurate. An eyewitness or participant's account of an event, written or recorded close in time to the event, should be reliable. Yet even a witness may have some bias or vested interest that would cause him to alter what he asserts to be true. Possible motives for such alteration must be considered by the examiner of the data. Also, a recollection of an event written fifty years later by a witness may not be as accurate as an account recorded when his memory was fresh.

Secondary data are often considered to be more reliable if compiled some time after an event. Conflicting stories may be resolved or at least explained by an investigator, and an event somewhat removed in time may be easier to view objectively. But in the case of secondary information, the person recording that information is not a witness—he heard it from somebody else.

Either kind of data may be laced with interpretation by the person doing the recording. And that person may in fact be incorrect in what he thinks he sees or hears. And, again, the word "incorrect" only indicates a type of judgment made by yet other people looking at what the person said.

Scientists prefer to deal with primary data (even if that is a fossil). Humanists use both in varying mixture.

Whatever data is used, the way it is handled by the user often differs. A natural scientist tends to use the kind of logic called inductive. That is, a common part of scientific method is to observe many instances of something happening a particular way (measuring the speed of light in all directions and doing it again and again); and if the "something" happens, or is observed, the same way each time, a scientist may assume with some degree of reliability that it will *always* happen that way. As long as it does, the statement of what happened is considered to describe a correct, reliable, general fact. This is one way of moving from evidence to proof.

Another way to look at this is that a sufficient amount of cogent, believable evidence *is* proof, or constitutes proof. Of course, "cogent" and "believable," as well as "reliable," "correct," and "sufficient," are only words to evaluate the opinions one holds, or that others hold.

The humanities tend to be deductive. They take a specific happening, combine it with other facts derived from other happenings, and draw inferences from them. (A majority of people in Hidalgo County speak Spanish; people in Hidalgo County who speak Spanish are of Mexican descent; therefore, the majority of people in Hidalgo County are of Mexican descent.) Deduction works well unless any part of the process is false—as in the example just used. Then, the whole construction turns out to be logically unsound, even though the truth of the conclusion may still be proven or "demonstrated" valid by other evidence. Conclusions in the humanities may be either specific, particular statements or simply generalities.

The social sciences—sociology, psychology, even a lot of education these days—are on the borderland of all this. They try to devise scientific conclusions from their data, which means that some workers in these fields try to establish general, reproducible facts through tests and experiments in the same manner as that used by physicists.

But this mid-ground makes little difference to a fact. In all disciplines, absolute fact frequently becomes or seems to become somewhat relative. (The physicist often will admit relative uncertainty the most readily, followed by the humanist, then the social scientist. . . .)[1]

Most statements can never be absolutely proven, particularly when they refer to events removed in time. There are, however, some statements recognized by so many people and supported by so much data that they are held as absolute truth. And some statements are true by definition: "I'm holding four marbles in my hand" or "All bachelors are unmarried." These are statements true by arbitrary definition. But everyone is aware that most of the statements of history (including many of the dates and names) are hardly definitions—they are questioned, changed, and reinterpreted in different centuries even when taken from the same data.

Indeed, most accepted beliefs in the humanities are inferences or opinions, but are documented so well that most people don't question them—or they are statements so obvious to common knowledge (or indeed so useful) that they almost never get questioned.

This is not a failure of the data. Natural scientists are faced with somewhat the same situation. They realize that it is impossible to describe, absolutely and completely, a physical state.

But this does not mean chaos for either physics or history. Enough can be known to describe a rational, dependable, predictable world for life as we know it. There's no practical reason to question the definition of "four" every day. A knowledge of past happenings, definitions, current consensus, and acceptability of things among one's neighbors—and what is in one's own head—is necessary for a life that is not repetitive, unreliable, or at times dangerous. If one remembers the "past" meaning of a red traffic light, one will probably not get flattened by a truck; if a nation remembers the past meaning of an atomic bomb blast, such an explosion might not easily happen again. But a person must consider and judge evidence—not just swallow "facts"—in order to live a productive or creative life.

One should be able to make some sort of judgment of evidence and consider how "facts" are supported. History may

[1] Obviously, author's opinion derived from experience. There are no other notes to this chapter because of the general nature of the discussion. Logic and the nature of proof have been considerations since the earliest recorded utterances of man.

The literatures of the philosophy of history, historiography, logic, and the character of language may now be almost endless. The following books would be a good few to read first (and from which much of this chapter is drawn):

Ayer, *Language, Truth & Logic*
Barzun, *The Modern Researcher*
Carr, *What Is History?*
Gottschalk, *Understanding History*
Walsh, *Philosophy of History*

Walsh and Carr are splendid places to start; Gottschalk and Barzun are practical handbooks; and Ayer gives a most incisive analysis of language, truth, and logic—exactly as his title indicates.

Epstein's "Pre-Columbian Old World Coins" is a good example of the handling of data. For fun, see Lamb's, "Science by Litigation." Concerning the phenomenon of "cult" archaeology, see Cole.

The question of what evidence is admissible in scientific reasoning is becoming quite heated in some areas, e.g. archaeology. In addition to Cole, the following works deal with the phenomena of what has been called "cult" archaeology and the nature of "popularizing" scientific not repeat itself totally in a useful or predictable way, yet a person can get along in the world a lot better if he has a knowledge of facts in the humanities and can judge those facts. Without them, a person could never even hope to understand his own age and himself. It is a question of efficiency, and the importance is direct. A person comes to know when one's newspaper or neighbor might be trusted. A person who can judge evidence can also present his own ideas more effectively to others.

Even beyond the reliability of the evidence, the motive of the source of data, the feelings and beliefs of the person doing the writing or talking must always be considered. Is there a reason for someone editing and choosing among the data; is there evidence of direct lying or alteration of data? Then, one should also consider the possibility of a person not following the urge of an obvious motive. One of the most common ways to cast doubt on a statement is to show that a reporter had a motive to "slant the facts"—whether he did so or not.

Naturally, the genuineness of documents needs to be considered, and this again may reflect a motive. Could such evidence be a forgery? Some scholars, needing a professional boost, have even created "hitherto unknown documents." Some newspapermen have done the same. And some humanists, while not making up material, so edit the data as to support only one interpretation; some just make careless errors; and some may be wonderfully accurate in all things.

Everyday life is the greatest of the humanities. Judgment is difficult in this field but important. When one hears that "our national security is in danger unless we revive the national draft" or "nuclear-powered electric plants are actually safe," one should consider whether the statement is defensible. Is it an inference or an opinion? Is it rational? And, further, does the statement make any difference? Then, if it does make a difference, how can the evidence be judged?

And in structure, the judgment of everyday questions is often the same as deciding whether an explorer by the name of Hwui Shan walked through North America about fifteen hundred years ago. That decision might not make any difference—the ability to make such a decision might be the most important talent a person can have.

theory (see the bibliography for full references):

Charles J. Cazeau and Stuart D. Scott Jr., in *Exploring the Unknown,* examine the phenomenon of "pseudoscientists" and provide a good discussion of the scientific method—with examples. They include a section on "ancient mariners" (21f).

William Sims Bainbridge's "Chariots of the Gullible" is a statistical look at von Daniken believers and non-believers, or, who is likely to believe what.

For another side of things, see Fell and Totten.

CLASSICAL REFERENCES
AND OLD MANUSCRIPTS

Stories about early Old World explorers going to the Americas from Europe and Africa are legion. There is almost no end to the accounts that mention early travelers making their way across the Atlantic, but—much before A.D. 1500—supporting evidence is a little scarce, to say the least. For each story, usually preserved in a single, old manuscript or an often-copied note, there is not a wealth of further evidence to indicate that the story is true. Evidence becomes speculative, and those who venture out on the seas of such speculation risk their professional reputation just as the early mariners constantly risked their lives.

Hubert Howe Bancroft, writing almost a century ago as one of the United States' most renowned historians, likened historical fact concerning early exploration to a coastline itself:

> The sixteenth century is a bluff coast line bounding the dark unnavigable sea of American antiquity. At a very few points along the long line headlands project slightly into the waters, affording a tolerable sure footing for a time, but terminating for the most part in dangerous reefs and quicksands over which the adventurous antiquarian may pass with much risk still farther from the firm land of written record, and gaze at the flickering mythical lights attached to buoys beyond.[1]

[1] Bancroft, vol. V, "The Native Races," 134-35.

33

Imaginary sea monster, 16th century

Those adventurous antiquarians, according to Bancroft who used the term in a beautifully insulting way, were false historians

who are continually dreaming they have found secure footing by routes previously unknown, from rock to rock through the midst of shifting sands . . . they carefully sift out such mythic traditions as fit their theories, converting them into incontrovertible facts, and reject all else as unworthy of notice. . . .[2]

[2] Ibid., 153.

Continuing his metaphor, Bancroft said that this kind of speculator was one who

steps out without hesitation from rock to rock over the deep waters; to him the banks of shifting quicksand, if somewhat treacherous about the edges, are firm land in the central parts; to him the faintest buoy-supported stars are a blaze of noonday sun; and only on the floating masses of sea-weed far out on the waters lighted up by dim phosphorescent reflections, does he admit that his footing is becoming insecure and the light grows faint.[3]

[3] Ibid., 154.

The style is that of academic contention of a century ago. The opinion is still most clear. Bancroft thought little of the speculative antiquarian. But he thought that the historian who engaged in speculation—properly labeled—was doing acceptable work, indeed even desirable work. In fact, after saying that he himself wanted to write carefully documented history, Bancroft went on to say:

I would pass beyond the firm land, spring from rock to rock, wade through shifting sands, swim to the farthest, faintest light, and catch at straws by the way;—yet not flatter myself while thus employed . . . that I am treading dry-shod on a wide, solid, and well-lighted highway.[4]

[4] Ibid., 154-55.

Bancroft knew the value of speculation and imagination, but the last phrase makes a great deal of difference. One should know what one stands upon. The stories concerning the first Old World arrivals traveling west to what became known as the Americas should be considered in the light of Bancroft's cautions. And in a hundred years of modern archaeological search, there are indeed few hard facts pointing to anyone—except the Vikings in Newfoundland in A.D. 1000—having made landfall in the Americas before 1492. Yet the disputed facts and the questions, the possibilities and probabilities, even admittedly unproven hints have spawned scores of books and articles.

The trouble that confronts an investigator today is that what record remains is most often an incomplete reference, a shattered clay tablet there, a folktale with perhaps a basis in fact here, or a manuscript that is only a fragment and perhaps quite literally moldy. But a few things do remain. There are stories concerning arrivals in the Americas by early sailors, priests, princes, merchants, soldiers, mercenaries, traders, pirates, and private citizens among other explorers of unknown intent, all bent on seeing what was beyond an ocean or perhaps accidentally blown the wrong way much too far.[5]

[5] For recent secondary collections, see Fiske, Boland, Fell, Crone, Gordon, McKern, Wauchope, Trento, Cohen, Riley, and Marschall.

Stories attesting, however unreliably, to a continent west of Europe and Africa have likewise been numerous for almost as long as man has written. Before becoming specific concerning Texas and the Gulf of Mexico region, a few general concerns can provide background for explorers to the Texas area and background for deciding one's position in Bancroft's terms.

People, some people, that is, of Europe, Africa, and the Near East always thought that there was a continent to the west or at least a collection of islands of great interest. These lands were not easily attainable. Their supposed distance, the dangers of the ocean, and the fact that few seemed to return from such a place made travel apparently risky.

To most European and African travelers, the far east and far west were either places one visited very rarely or were entirely mythical. The west, to the eyes of the European Old World, was the place where the sun set and thus was poetically a place of haven, life's end, or death. It was Hades to some or the location of the Isles of the Blest to others. It was even the suspected Atlantis, the drowned continent, among a host of other ideas that a great majority of people at one time or another firmly believed in.[6] These ideas were not usually based on stories of voyages, however, but were rather what had to be true to balance earlier ideas of western philosophy, religion, or geography.[7]

Yet lands beyond the Old World were also real places. Even at the time of classical Greek civilization, say 400 B.C., the world was known to be spherical.[8] Europe and North Africa and

[6] Benitez, 1-14; "Ancient Explorers," by J.V. Luce in Ashe, 53f; Plato's *Timaeus* and *Critias* present not only the Atlantis myth, but also the former speaks of the continent to the far west; Herrmann, 156-62.

[7] As an example, see Plutarch (Goodwin's translation, Loeb), vol. V.

[8] Ashe, 15-21.

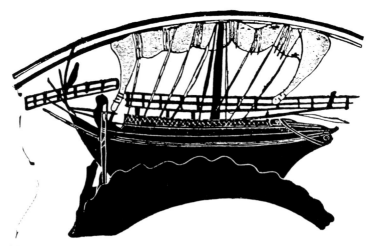

Athenian merchant ship, c. 500 B.C., copied from a vase painting

Asia represented the known world (for the peoples of these places), and this area was clearly on one side of a sphere. Erathosthenes, in about 200 B.C., measured the correct size of the earth, and Crates of Pergamum built a globe in the second century B.C. showing the philosophically necessary but unknown continents to the west. Other maps (such as that composed by the Roman Macrobius in the fourth century A.D.) represented the faces of the world as two hemispheres, one adorned with relatively crude drawings of Europe, Asia, and at least part of Africa.[9] The other side was, in some of the more complete books of geography, simply a blank circle. For this reason, the second side was often left out. Book producers then had just as much reason as those today to save money, and why have a blank circle?

Thus, people looking at the picture—particularly those who could not read the accompanying Latin text—were unaware that the simple-looking circle represented half of a globe, and so they assumed that the illustrated picture was of a flat earth.[10] In the minds of the not-so-learned (most of Europe's population at that time), the earth became a flat disc.

But even if some people knew the earth was round, there were other problems. It was still not easy to go to the other

[9] Crone, 2.

[10] The "common people" did indeed see maps—in churches, for example, see Crone, 2-3.

side. The earth consisted of various belts of climate. The northern part was obviously too cold for habitation, and the zone at the equator was just as obviously hot enough to set ablaze the sails of any ship taken there by an overzealous captain or hot enough to burn the sandals off of anyone intrepid enough to try to walk that far south in Africa. A perilous world for travelers, indeed.

But the spherical shape also guaranteed that if there was any land further south of the equator, it should be temperate. Likewise, there would be two pleasant zones on the other side of the earth.[11] This was, of course, only theoretically known. The catch was that the equator and its impassable heat bisected the earth one way, and a fearful ocean split the earth the other way.

[11] Diodorus (Oldfather translation, Loeb, 19), I. V. 19; Crone, 3.

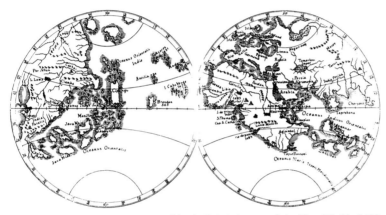

Martín Behaim's map of the New World, 1492

Europe, Asia, and North Africa were confined. There was even a moral question as to whether man should try to cross into another zone.

But there is a curious thing about some men and women. They will often try to go precisely where their reason (correctly or not) says they can not or should not go. Now the motive may indeed be obstinace or curiosity, gold or spices, wine or women, or men for that matter; but they will go. And the motives vary. When Queen Hatshepsut of Egypt ordered an expedition through the Red Sea about 1500 B.C., she sailed for the usual gold and spices, wine and curiosity—but also for cosmetics and men.[12]

So even though the heat of an equator promised to vaporize boats and the oceans to mysteriously swallow ships, there were mariners who dared the horizons and overland caravan leaders who steered by the stars.[13]

The first known mariners in the Atlantic—the Africans, Phoenicians, and Carthaginians—found it a strange place.

[12] Marx, "Egyptian Shipping," *passim;* Anon., "The Queen Who Would Be Different" (a romanticized version, but fun); Ashe, 71; and Sølver, "Egyptian Shipping of About 1500 B.C."—by far the best.

[13] Benitez, chap. I, for a romantic picture of exploring the unknown

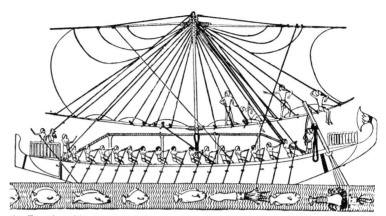

An Egyptian ship, c. 1600 B.C., from a rock carving at Deir el-Bahri

and the dependence of exploration on myth. And by this time, there is apparently no question that there had been ships capable of sailing oceans for at least forty-five hundred years or that they could sail to windward. See Verwey on the last point, who quotes Aristotle's *Mechanica*, 8.

14 Al-Idrisi, *passim;* Galvano (Galvão), *passim;* Morison, *Portuguese;* Riley, eds., particularly sec. 14, 274.

15 Herodotus, iv. 41.

16 Babcock, 1-10; King, 38-40; Herodotus, i. In spite of numerous stories, the Carthaginians, at least in literature, held that no one had taken a ship across the Atlantic. But perhaps they were also hiding a secret. See Heeren, i. 178.

17 Crone, 8.

18 The peculiarities on some maps had very specific purposes, such as political display. Herodotus, v. 49; Cassidy, 37-39; Babcock, Harrisse, and Brown, *passim*.

Unlike the Mediterranean, the ocean had obvious tides, a very uncertain western shore (if any at all), massive storms, and was undoubtedly filled with monsters.

But not everything was against them. The waters could be sailed like other water, and the weather and shoals, landfalls and passages could be learned.[14] Phoenician mariners circumnavigated Africa in the sixth century B.C., about two thousand years before the Portuguese Dias rounded the Cape of Good Hope in 1488 — but in the other direction.[15] Later, the Phoenicians and their kinsmen from their main colony, Carthage, sailed out of the Mediterranean to the west, setting up colonies in Africa and the Atlantic coast of Spain and Portugal, and visiting Britain and various Atlantic islands.[16]

In the course of all this, more than a few boats were blown about considerably, and interesting stories began to accumulate about a rather large land to the west. Some of the stories were certainly powered by myth. The early maps, charts, and accounts were fed not only by the philosophical tradition of a western land, but also by the poetic tradition of mythical lands which were places of paradise, rest, and haven gained after a life (or a voyage) of trouble.[17] In time, Hades — the more somber western tradition — was forgotten.

Islands and shorelines flickered on the early maps limited only by the cartographers' imagination.[18] When one is drawing a map, blank space is both very boring and professionally embarrassing. Unexplored inland areas became peopled with strange animals, speculative mountains, specious hermits, and questionable cities; reaches of unknown ocean were broken with complicated islands, erotic mermaids, colorful wind roses, and dreadful sea monsters.[19] Accounts of voyages west which accompanied the charts ran the gamut from logical-sounding narratives to the science fiction of the day.[20]

[19] Among the decorations the wind roses were the only things perhaps meant to be helpful. These were the eight- and sixteen-pointed designs that set the style for compass cards. Often highly colored, they radiated a set of lines over the chart surface before latitude and longitude lines were common. Of more use to mariners who navigated by dead reckoning, they were mildly useful for estimating compass bearings.

[20] Morison, *Portuguese,* 18; Collier, *passim.*

phoenician sailors
and yellow cats

The Phoenicians provide many stories of ocean voyages and overland explorations, but whether they came to the New World centuries ago is still a matter of controversy that is heating up academically rather than cooling down.[1] That the Phoenicians were outstanding mariners is well known. It is not quite so commonly known that they were also experienced land navigators and caravaneers who took their bearings from the stars.[2]

Their homelands were the eastern shores of the Mediterranean, present-day Lebanon and Syria; but they were respected as traders on land and sea in most of the Old World.[3] They maintained their position as the foremost navigators from about 1200 B.C. to 146 B.C. when Rome sacked their colonial city of Carthage. By that year Carthage was already cut off from the eastern Phoenician lands.[4]

Calling themselves "Canaanites," a one-time Mediterranean synonym for "merchants," the Phoenicians were known to have sailed on the Atlantic and Indian oceans, as well as the Mediterranean and Red seas.[5] Although they operated extensive caravan routes overland to the east, they are remembered more often as sailors with style and skill all their own. They were one of very few groups of seafaring men who allowed women on board merchant ships.[6] It is also thought that the Phoeni-

[1] Anon., "Was Hanno discoverer"; Boland, *They All Discovered America;* Johnston, *passim.*

[2] Strabo (Loeb, I, 9 and I, 177), I.1.6 and I.3.2.

[3] Herodotus, i. 1 and iii. 113.

[4] General: Moscati, Herm, *passim.* Herodotus, Diodorus, and Strabo along with the Old Testament are some of the older secondary references. The Loeb edition is well indexed, and the later references provide subject citations to general Mediterranean history.

[5] Diodorus (Oldfather translation, Loeb, I: 145f), v. 19-20; Kan, "De

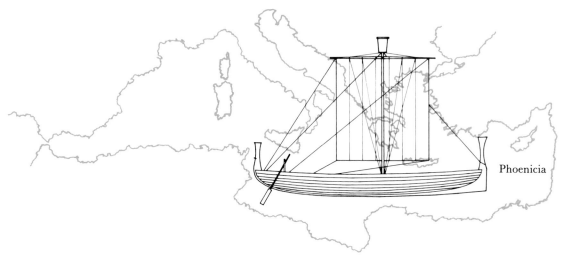

Phoenician merchantman

Periplous"; for the ships, see Anderson, Romola, and Harden.

[6] Herodotus, i. 5.

[7] Todd, "Cats and Commerce." Phoenicians apparently liked orange and black cats. The Vikings liked white.

[8] See Appendix 2. It is also notable that the Greeks were fond of pointing out that not *all* women aboard Phoenician ships were there by choice. The Phoenicians (and others of the eastern Mediterranean) did not strictly refute this statement but did point out that even this category of women were loath to leave once aboard.

[9] Herodotus, v. 58.

[10] Herodotus, iii. 136.

[11] For supposed Phoenician finds on the east coast of the United States, see Lossing, 632-35; Boland, *passim*.

[12] But see Johnston for a defense of their discovery of the Americas — from the west; Mallery, 211f.

cians deliberately took cats aboard their trading ships to control the rats, thereby not incidentally taking cats all over the known world. In particular, the yellow-colored tomcat seems to have been a Phoenician favorite.[7]

Most of the existing accounts of their voyages and overland travels were written by others — notably the Greeks[8] — for, even though the Phoenicians gave their alphabet to the western world, few of their own narratives apparently have survived.[9] Either they deliberately did not write of their voyages, perhaps to keep a monopoly on their routes, or modern archaeologists simply have not been lucky enough to find tablets bearing their stories. The Phoenicians are known to have made maps, but apparently none survived.[10] They also kept business records, some of which have been found, and did inscribe graffiti, notices of ownership and boundaries, religious inscriptions, and announcements of voyages almost everywhere they went.[11]

The Mediterranean area is fairly well endowed with short Phoenician inscriptions. Inscriptions that *may* be Phoenician have been discovered elsewhere — but with little other evidence of Phoenician occupation.[12] As languages (and governments) changed in the Mediterranean area, Phoenician came to be written not only in Phoenician characters but also in early Greek characters (which were actually "modern" Phoenician) and Hebrew. Some writers even mixed alphabets in a single inscription, which gives pause to modern scholars.

Variously written, Phoenician inscriptions are found most places the Phoenicians went. Old World inscriptions create no other trouble than occasional difficulty in transcription. Similar inscriptions in the New World usually give rise to one word: fake.

A long inscription was found in Brazil a century ago, which, when allegedly translated, told the story of a voyage from the Red Sea to the Brazilian coast in the tenth century B.C.[13] Most scholars were not slow to label the original as fake and the translation a hoax. These authorities generally believe that sailors, before Columbus, were self-confined to sailing along coastlines. A very few saw the story as a logical extension of the accepted Phoenician voyages.

[13] Herrmann, 211f.

Phoenician galley

Similar inscriptions have turned up on the east coast of North America, as well as inland. Two such inscriptions have been found in the drainage of the Rio Grande, one in New Mexico, the other from the Big Bend area of Texas. Even the few authorities who say the inscriptions are genuine ancient script disagree on what language is represented.

The New Mexico stone is inscribed in what appears to be early Hebrew in a Phoenician alphabet of a form used about 1000 B.C. in the eastern Mediterranean. The stone was discovered in a very remote place, which creates a puzzle. If it is a hoax, it is a well-hidden one.[14] If genuine, it means a Phoenician was exploring the Rio Grande some twenty-five hundred years ago.

Quite a way downriver, within the present boundaries of Big Bend National Park, a perhaps related find was made.[15] In January of 1962 Charles and Bernice Nickles and Reva and Donald Uzzell, related families, were vacationing together. Their tour took them to the Hot Springs area of the park at the junction of Tornillo Creek and the Rio Grande just above Boquillas.

[14] Williams and Pepper, 22-26. For an alleged transcription, see Perkins, *passim*, who maintains the writer was Greek. Recent, perhaps more scholarly, comment can be found in the *Occasional Publications of the Epigraphic Society:* "The Los Lunas Inscription," vol. 10, no. 237; "The Los Lunas Stone," vol. 10, no. 238; and "A Decipherment of the Los Lunas Decalogue Inscription," vol. 10, no. 239.

[15] McGee, *passim*.

In 1962, twenty years after the land, bought by the State of Texas, had been presented to the national government as a park, Hot Springs was a collection of abandoned buildings. Just after the turn of the century, however, it was a flourishing, privately owned spa. At its height it was a small settlement of a few families, a trading post, motor court, campground, and bathhouse. The area was frequented by those who came to drink—and bathe in—the natural mineral waters that come to the surface at a comfortable 105°F. Today, the bathhouse and the main hot spring are almost gone, swept away and almost covered by the eroding Rio Grande.

The area has been known at least since local Indians scraped out a depression to catch the restorative waters. Many later travelers stopped to refresh themselves—whether accidentally passing or deliberately visiting the area.[16]

When the Nickles and Uzzell families visited Hot Springs, Donald Uzzell climbed the cliffs on the side of Tornillo Creek across from the old settlement. Some thirty feet above the creek bed, he found a fragmented clay tablet protected in a small niche. The pieces were neatly stacked and bore strange, incised characters. Scrambling down the cliff, he reassembled the tablet, and Charles Nickles took photographs of the curious writing. Unable to decipher the markings, the group took the artifact to park headquarters and left it with a ranger for safekeeping and further study. The families were curious about the strange writing, however, and offered photographs to several authorities including Dr. Cyclone Covey of Wake Forest University and Dr. Cyrus Gordon of Brandeis University.

At first no one could decipher the markings, although the most favorable opinions classified it as a phonetic language, at least related to early Greek, written in a blend of Judean Hebrew and Sidonian Phoenician alphabets. Such strange combinations are found in Europe but are not exactly common in Texas. The least complimentary comments called the markings those of a Mexican goatherd. Yet the marks do include Phoenician characters that such a person would probably not have known nor have made up by chance.

One theory suggested by Covey, that a party of Phoenicians might have descended the Rio Grande (leaving the New Mexico and Texas inscriptions near the waterway), is, in the face of a lack of further evidence, hard to believe. In any case, Phoenicians would not have been confined to the waterway since they were also experienced overland navigators; but the route would have been a logical one to or from the sea. It provides a supply of water and is beautiful.

[16] The Rio Grande (from at least the Big Bend area south to Ciudad Acuña) is bordered by a number of hot springs, arising from some geologically unspecified source, many large enough to accommodate a tired party of fifteen or so, others only large enough for two tired feet.

So far only one scholar has offered a complete transcription of the tablet: Dr. Barry Fell claims that the script and language are very grammatical, centuries-old Iberian, not Phoenician, and that the message is a supplication to Ahura-Mazda to protect a small group of Iberian Zoroastrians during a plague.[17] Such opinions are questioned—or ignored—by most scholars.

In any case, the motive for a hoax seems thin indeed because the Tornillo cliff at the Rio Grande is an unlikely place for someone to hide something that was intended to be found— particularly on the wrong side of a former spa. And the recent finders had no apparent motive for a hoax. A clay tablet, or even a mud tablet, could last for centuries, and the lack of agreement concerning the script may not be evidence that it is a fake. In fact, if it were a hoax, it would be more likely that the script could be more easily read.

The original tablet is no longer in existence. The ranger, to whom the find was first presented, later said—in contrast to other observers—that the inscription was not on clay or rock but appeared to be on recent mud such as that which forms along Tornillo Creek after every heavy rain. He and other park personnel agreed that the tablet showed no signs of age, again, unlike other opinions. It was carefully kept, however, until it disintegrated. So the story goes.

[17] Fell, personal communication; *Saga America,* 164-65.

Tornillo Creek at Hot Springs, the Big Bend

Title page of Regimiento de Navegacion, *Pedro de Medina, 1543*

A Few Inscriptions:
Lost Greeks and
Wandering Romans

Inscriptions and carvings, supposed Phoenician or not, are almost always so brief and usually so questionable as to be unacceptable as dependable evidence of the presence of early explorers. No inscription of any Old World language in the New World, before 1492, is accepted by the majority of scholars today. Indeed, to give credence to any such inscription is taken as being purely illogical.[1] Some inscriptions, some stories, are fun to consider, however. There are always a few that because of their association or their similarity to genuine records create the impression that they might be legitimate records of explorers.

A generation ago Esau Nelson found a rather strange carved stone in the canyon of the Pecos River. It was mainly floral in design, which might indicate that it was the practice work of an early stonecutter. Yet it was far away from any logical place for stonecutting. It bore the inscriptions "D'AVE" (too neatly spaced out to read *Dave)* and "Ph.Coni" or "Phi Coni" (carved a little more questionably). Now on display at Alamo Village in Brackettville, no one knows why it was carved.

And there the story should stop, and does, but for the possibility (the records have never been confirmed) that an Italian sculptor called "Coni" left the Mediterranean world in A.D. 1165

[1] See Cole, all articles cited.

[2] Such was the local story told in the past, personal correspondence, Wheelis, 1968.

[3] Fell, *passim;* Farley, personal correspondence.

[4] Fleming, 16.

for parts unknown and never returned.[2] And there the story really does stop.

Naturally this is probably a coincidence of name. It is the type of evidence that isn't. And there are other mysterious carvings like this in Texas—such as the stone head found near Schulenburg a decade ago—but they are unsigned and are surely only reminders that stonemasons and tombstone carvers need to practice.

These are instances of things found without any other records concerning them and with no associated evidence of where they came from. They are items without provenance—not found buried in dateable sites nor capable of being independently dated by methods known at present. Some inscriptions, however, appear in groups, a factor that is itself a type of evidence.

North of the Red River, in Oklahoma, a bewildering array of short inscriptions has been found. Many stones examined by Gloria Farley of Heavener are thought to bear traces of Phoenicians or Libyans who visited and perhaps settled the land more than two thousand years ago.[3] Such thinking is again the belief of very few people.

Why these Mediterranean peoples might have been near the Red River area at that time is absolutely unknown. If they were there, what they were doing is not strange at all, because people have always done the same—they were exploring and perhaps settling. The inscriptions—some of them deciphered as Punic, the language of the Cadiz Phoenicians; or Ogham, a script of the European Celts; or Libyan boundary markers—if found in another part of the world, would cause no raised eyebrows. Since related items include Carthaginian coins, a carved female figure identified as the Phoenician goddess Tanit, and a transcription of Pharaoh Akhenaten's Hymn to the Sun—and since these items relate to the history of two thousand and more years ago—eyebrows are raised indeed, most of them skeptically.

Yet the items do not appear to be part of a recently lost collection and are at least interesting, although there is no further evidence of authenticity.[4] Most scholars dismiss the finds as a hoax or as terribly misguided readings of unknown marks on rocks. The most liberal theories hold that these eastern Mediterranean peoples voyaged across the Atlantic, entered the Gulf of Mexico, and made their way up the Mississippi and Red rivers. The most conservative opinions are that the marks are those of recent settlers and that the translators of the marks are simply fools.

Paintings and etchings on rocks (pictographs and petroglyphs) in Texas have excited the curiosity of many. Existing

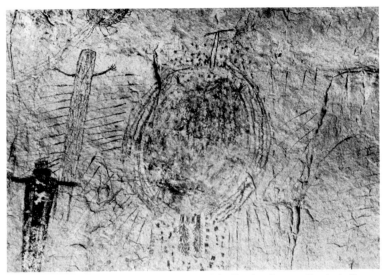

Pictograph in Panther Cave at Seminole Canyon

mainly in the drier climate of west Texas where rock overhangs and ledges provide convenient surfaces, the paintings and carvings depict events, religious ceremonies, hunting records, and a variety of things only guessed at today. Their ages are simply unknown.[5] And they are presumably the work of native American Indians.

However, there are designs that could be from other hands or by Indians who had seen non-Indian things. There is one possible representation of a Phoenician craft with raised, protected gunwales;[6] lines that can be read as European Ogham script, but which are certainly not;[7] engravings which could be read as runes, but are usually interpreted as Indian "tally marks";[8] and some miscellaneous markings which seem translatable.

The most well known in the latter category is an inscription on the Rio Grande which has been read as a message in Libyan and Ogham attesting to a crew that took shelter under the rock overhang during a trip from the Mediterranean area about 800 B.C.[9] If that reading is correct, it is a hint that the Rio Grande was used as a route of exploration by hitherto unknown explorers.

An alleged Ogham inscription in Stephens County has been claimed to be of Celtic origin, many centuries old, and to indicate a camping place arranged with the permission of the local Indians.[10]

All of these interpretations are simply items of derision to most people.

Scores of miles of river rock overhangs still may contain messages, although today some of the writing is under the waters of modern Amistad Reservoir. The route up (or down) the Rio

[5] Those with Puebloan influence are tentatively dated from A.D. 900 to 1500 and are considered relatively recent. Kirkland and Newcomb, 217.

[6] Pecos River cave 1, Kirkland and Newcomb, 76.

[7] Panther Cave, author's examination; Kirkland and Newcomb, 66; and Lehmann Rock Shelter, Kirkland and Newcomb, 159. The question of brief inscriptions and what their transcription and translation should be is a thorny question. Ogham is one of the hardest since it, as a script, may phonetically express many languages (some without the benefit of vowels). Some markings, demonstrably not Ogham, can be transcribed as Ogham. See, in addition to Barry Fell's *America B.C.*, Greene, Kelly, and Fraser.

[8] Paint Rock site and Panther Cave, author's field work; also examples in Kirkland and Newcomb, 62.

[9] Fell, *America B.C.*, 185.

[10] Fell, "Stephens County," 107.

Grande is a logical one for exploration. One of the most common sailing routes from Europe — that followed by Columbus and the Spanish — drops down south in the Atlantic into the winds leading to the Caribbean. Once there, the route leads between Yucatán and Cuba, then into harbors like Veracruz or to the major rivers: Pánuco, Rio Grande, Mississippi.

And there are stories attesting that such a Caribbean route was followed — at times accidentally — to the New World before the Christian era. One of the most interesting, recorded by Pausanias, concerns the Greeks.[11] He tells the story of a shipload of Greeks who sailed out into the Atlantic more than

[11] Pausanias, 1, 23.5-6; and there are even stories of the Phoenicians and Greeks approaching the Americas from the Pacific side, Gladwin, *passim;* and note the enthusiastic support by Texas Greeks, in Anon., "Greeks First to Discover America."

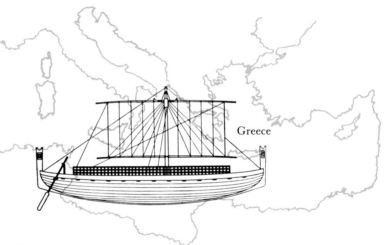

Greece

Greek trader

two thousand years ago. Caught in a storm, they were blown far to the west, where they sailed among islands of large size. On one of these they were surprised by the sudden appearance of men dressed only in tails similar to horses. These men naturally reminded the Greeks of their tradition of satyrs.

These strange natives immediately spotted the women aboard ship. Pausanias does not state whether these women were passengers or servants. The "satyrs," without uttering a sound, swarmed up to the ship and attempted to carry off the women.

Exactly how they did this Pausanias does not make clear, but the effort was enough to scare the Greek sailors. Without further ado, they simply shoved a "barbarian" woman overboard onto the island and made good their escape while the "satyrs" outraged the woman in a variety of ways amazing even to the sophisticated Greeks.

In this case at least, it was the navigator who brought the story back to Greece. Euphemus was obviously watching more than the position of the sun and the coastline during the affray. He lived up to his name by avoiding most of the unpleasant details of the story.

An interesting fact is that such a costume, a tail, was recorded in the later years of Spanish exploration in the Caribbean. Some writers cite natives attired with detachable horse-like tails, who were noted for satyr-like actions.[12]

But if Greeks left any inscriptions on Texas rocks, they are yet to be found.[13]

Stories about the Romans are cited also, although most of them concern Christian Romans who were forced to leave the early Empire.

The Romans were aware of land to the west; at least there are references to it in the literature. Plutarch, in the first century A.D., wrote of a continent a thousand miles or so to the west of Britain.[14] Men had visited the place, the Greeks had put a colony there, and it was quite possible to sail there — so it was said. The account, laced with gods in residence and unlikely geography, nevertheless contains what may be evidence of an actual visit. The all-night summer twilight of northern lands is recorded, for example.

In A.D. 64, during the reign of the Emperor Nero, a great fire swept Rome. Although it almost died out a couple of times, it was kept going by agents of someone. It was even rumored that Nero himself wanted to burn the city, so he could build a new one in his own honor. A scapegoat had to be found.

The people who were eventually blamed were the Christians, at that time members of a young and disreputable religious sect. Many Christians were killed in the persecutions that followed, but some managed to escape — and some who escaped literally took ship for as far as they could go.

[12] Hyde, 162; Lafitau, I:105; I:1-2, 31f.

[13] Although rumors do exist of "Greek" inscriptions — author's field work and interviews in Pine Springs and Marathon, Texas.

[14] Plutarch, "Of the Face Appearing Within the Orb of the Moon," Plutarch's *Morals,* 281f. The distance given is five days' sail plus five thousand stadia.

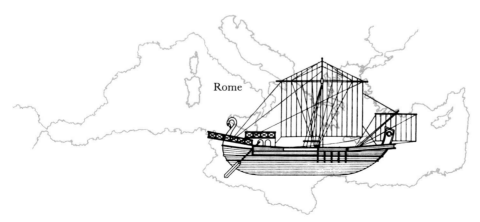

Rome

Roman merchantman

[15] Heine-Geldern, 118.

[16] Heine-Geldern, 117.

[17] Boland, 47f.
[18] Mallery, *passim.*

[19] Williams and Pepper, 13f; Covey, *passim.*

Nor was this reason the only one for Romans to go beyond the borders of the Empire. Romans and Roman trade goods went east to India and China and may have gone west.[15] Roman trade was exceptionally strong through the early fifth century.

In the Americas some evidence has come to light that would indicate at least accidental contact if not deliberate trade. A small terra-cotta head, identified as Roman, was found recently under undisturbed pre-Columbian pyramid paving in Mexico.[16] Evidence of early ironworking has been found in Virginia, along with related artifacts that could be Roman, near the Roanoke River.[17] Parallel ironworking sites have been claimed in Ohio that could be a thousand years old.[18] And apparent evidence of a Roman colony called Terra Calalus has been found in the vicinity of Tucson, Arizona.[19] The latter, labeled as a complete fraud by most investigators, is said to have been a colony of some seven hundred Romans who, after sailing through the Pillars of Hercules, were blown far across the sea. According to an

Romantic drawing of Roman galleys in harbor

inscription found at the site, they sailed for a long time to a new land. They landed, and walked northwest through a wild and new countryside to a desert. This route would be across Texas, which is in accord with the idea that Texas is an eternal crossroads. The artifacts at the site, however, are undocumented. They consist of swords, crosses, a cast of a head, all made of a lead alloy hardened with antimony. The items were, by some stories, found in absolutely undisturbed caliche deposits, assuring their age. Other accounts, however, say the finds were made from automobile tire balancing weights, then planted with the original spade marks left visible to later excavators.

With such controversy, no proof is possible. Most scholars would say no serious consideration is required.

In Texas one unusual find concerns a coin—a Roman follis, minted in London in A.D. 313-314, and found in an Indian mound presumably undisturbed for at least the last nine hundred years.[20] The find is already called a "known and admitted hoax" by some investigators. But even if such a find were genuine, it might actually have no real significance.

It is important to note that such a coin would not by itself indicate Roman-American Indian trade or contact. The coin might simply have been interesting to Indians. It might have been found in the wreckage of a ship blown across the Atlantic—or Pacific—and passed between Indians in the Americas only as a curiosity. Shipwrecks might have brought coins but otherwise have had no real effect on American Indian culture.

Most finds of ancient coins in the Americas were certainly lost by later collectors.[21] A single coin if found in an undisturbed Indian mound would be harder to explain, but in itself would lack significance.

Some curious things in Texas rise to the level of the fantastic. Several peculiar "giant man tracks" are found in limestone rock, exposed by rivers—rock far too old for contemporary theories of the development of man.[22]

One well-preserved series of footprints is in the bedrock of the Paluxy River in Somerville County. They are next to well-preserved tracks of a trachodon of the Mesozoic Era—thought to be far too early for the existence of any man. The humanoid tracks, all about twenty-one inches long, have a stride of seven feet, easily twice that of modern man. Dr. Bull Adams, familiar with the dinosaur tracks of the Glen Rose area, argued in an earlier day that the human-like tracks were those of a giant sloth. Others, such as Dr. C.N. Dougherty, call attention to the perfect form of the footprints which would never be questioned if they were not so large and not preserved in limestone—limestone seventy million years old.[23]

If the tracks were human, they would certainly be those of the earliest Texan—but probably not an explorer.

But aside from footprints, aside from myth, marks on rocks are interesting in two ways. First, their very existence is interesting. There *are* strange and unexplained inscriptions in Texas which are either the messages or graffiti of earlier travelers, or the occasional occupation of recent travelers with a flair for old languages, or planned frauds, or coincidences.

Second, it is significant, when deciding about authenticity, to consider that the inscriptions not only are difficult or

[20] Watkins, *passim;* Epstein, *passim.*

[21] Epstein, *passim.*

[22] Tolbert, "Track of Man-like Giant."

[23] Dougherty, *passim.*

[24] Indeed, it is more than just a matter of humor perhaps that a recent computerized bill received from a leading gasoline credit company bore strange marks curiously like written Ogham down one side. This accidental Ogham could be phonetically transcribed to make fairly good nonsense statements. If it had been cut into a rock, it might have been taken as a message done some centuries ago.

impossible to date but also can mean different things. Whether they are "authentic" or not, they can be interpreted in different ways by different investigators. Chance markings can be mistranslated, and genuine inscriptions could be unrecognized. One should take the more simple of multiple interpretations—a tenet of western natural science.

Ambiguous, or dual, interpretation of data is an interesting facet of human understanding. Such possibility is significant in human experience from fields such as information theory to forms of art. It is a critical concern when dealing with fragmentary data.[24]

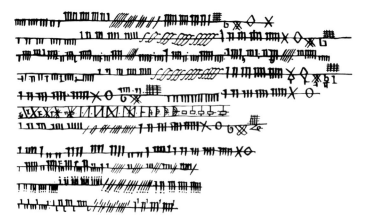

Ogham from the Book of Ballymote

LOST TRIBES AND ATLANTIS

W orth only passing comment is the unprovable collection of theories which, most arising in the last century, strive to connect the American Indians with the lost tribes of Israel or with the former inhabitants of the mysterious continent of Atlantis.[1] These theories are discounted today, although they had great currency in earlier years, notably before the floor of the Atlantic Ocean was substantially sounded and charted. For a time the Sargasso Sea, the great swirl of North Atlantic current in which not only sargasso seaweed but also sailing ships can be becalmed, was thought to be shallow water. In earlier centuries it was believed to be only a few feet deep and filled with such masses of seaweed that a person could actually walk on the surface. This, some people thought, was surely the site of Atlantis, perhaps at one time virtually a land bridge between Europe and the Americas which sank in a cataclysm eons ago. Since the mapping of the Atlantic basin, it is held by most geologists that the floor of the Atlantic has never been an elevated continent.

In a similar vein, the prophet Joseph Smith in the first half of the last century issued the *Book of Mormon* which traces some native American cultures back to Mediterranean peoples.[2] So far, such statements depend upon divine revelation and not on scientifically verifiable fact. This is not to say that such a theory

[1] Ignatius Donnelly, in his *Atlantis: The Antediluvian World,* says that there were (in the 1880's) over five thousand works concerning Atlantis in twenty languages. There are probably twice that today. They include ideas as specific as the supposed similarity between Atlantis's presumed capital city and the Cortés map of Mexico-Tenochtitlan (Spence, *The Problem of Atlantis*) to the general speculation that the southeast United States is actually Atlantis, mostly still high and dry (Mertz, *Atlantis, Dwelling Place of the Gods*). Aside from noting claims like Donnelly's that Atlanteans "populated the shores of the Gulf of Mexico," there is no reason to consider such stories here.

[2] Ashe, 9; Silverberg, 88-96.

may not be objectively true, but it does mean that any such theory is not yet provable, is not yet verifiable by external evidence, and is not capable of being scientifically discussed. One simply has the choice of believing in the theory or statement, or not believing, as one wishes. In any case, these theories do not concern those who can be called explorers.

Mermaid of the eighteenth century

Legendary Welsh dragon

A Churchman and a Prince
7

Two travelers who do qualify, if curiously, as real explorers are a churchman and a prince. Their narratives are quite unproven but are believed by many. The first is St. Brendan, an Irish man of the church born at Tralee around A.D. 490. He had a busy life filled with church activities, but he is also known for one or more voyages into the Atlantic. Most of the activities of Brendan's life, founding monasteries, for example, are believed without question as given in ninth, tenth, and eleventh century records. And in most of these cases, secondary evidence is available. However, Brendan's Atlantic voyages are questioned rather closely.

The most liberal interpretation of the *Navigatio Sancti Brendani,* a Latin manuscript work of about A.D. 800-1000, is that it records one or more voyages which took Brendan through the North Atlantic from the Arctic to the Caribbean.[1]

One might at first question why an early Irish priest would sail the Atlantic. In fact, many people did so then. Ireland, in the centuries after the removal of the Roman government from England, for a time became a land of renowned learning and dynamic Christianity. Even so, many an Irish churchman felt the desire for isolation — a need for a place secure from secular influences where one could meditate in peace, pray, endure hard-

[1] See Ashe, 21-47; Chapman and Severin are the most liberal of the interpreters of the voyage.

ships in partial atonement for sin, and perhaps retire. The rocky islands off the north coast of Britain served this purpose, as did Iceland and possibly Greenland. The Norse not only had legends that the Irish preceded them to the northern isles but also gave accounts of continually finding Irish priests in the most isolated and unlikely places.[2]

That the voyages west were possible is clear.[3] The Irish had boats made of ox hides, oak-bark tanned, oiled with wool grease, and stretched over wooden frames, which were quite seaworthy and capable of carrying up to twenty men. How early they used wooden boats is unknown.

In any case, the Irish did to some degree sail the Atlantic and did to a great degree inject a mix of geographical references into European literature from the sixth century on. These stories, like any heroic tales, tend to congregate around leading characters, no matter who actually did what. Most of the stories of voyages gathered around St. Brendan—who was soon known as "the Navigator"—and became part of his quest westward for an Earthly Paradise. In fact, his story is a collection of the best parts of all that is remembered about early voyages, Irish and otherwise,[4] stuck together into an occasionally incoherent narrative.

An alleged incident from Brendan's voyage . . .

Specific details are plentiful. Brendan, for at least one voyage, used a wooden boat capable of carrying sixty people (far in advance of any other evidence of wooden boats in Ireland). He sailed beyond the known bounds of a large ocean and described events, islands, and lands which range from the fantastic to the probable.

[2] The western "Great Ireland" or "white men's island" is mentioned in the *Landnamabok,* the *Saga of Erik the Red,* and in the *Eyrbyggia Saga* as well as in the works of Al-Idrisi, the Arab geographer. Unlike some references in these works, "Great Ireland" appears to refer to a literal continent somewhere west. Whether it was a land settled by the Irish, or occasioned by Irish monks, or pure fiction, is unknown. The thread of reference runs through many an extant record. See also Crone, 10f. For the Brendan manuscript and comments on his life and the propensities of Irish churchmen, see Selmer, *Navigatio Sancti Brendani Abbatis.*

[3] Severin, *passim;* for the boat construction, 27f. For the history of the somewhat related coracles, see Hornell.

[4] Irish writers were also aware of the classical Greek and Latin references to western worlds.

The most interesting details come from a voyage ascribed to about A.D. 550. Brendan sails to well-known and easily identified places, such as the Faeroes. He describes sheep which, according to other records, were in fact introduced there but not until many generations after Brendan. The compiler of the story evidently included facts from times well after the life of Brendan. The *Navigatio* may be thought of as a compendium of maritime knowledge, however confused, from someone writing about the year A.D. 950.

Other places allegedly visited by Brendan include islands and lands in a tropical setting which sounds like the Caribbean. He describes exotic fruits, beautiful islands, and clear seas such as are in the Bahamas or along the western Florida coast.[5] In passing to these places and on his return, he describes rather poetically what could be the Sargasso Sea, icebergs, and the volcanoes of Iceland.

[5] Interpreted by some (Crone, 16) as water in a Norwegian fiord, however.

Nova typis *frontispiece*

Brendan even finds the Earthly Paradise but says little about it. Further, he does land somewhere and take a forty-day expedition into the heart of the country. The finding of an Earthly Paradise was not taken lightly for centuries. Columbus, many years later, held in part the same desire, naming a South American river the Gihon (from Genesis II, 13) and saying he thought that South America might include the Paradise. Both Brendan and Columbus, among many others, not only knew that the earth was round but also surmised that the route west might lead to other things than spices. The way west might lead to China, but it might also lead to the fading medieval dream of a paradise on earth.[6]

[6] Ashe, 39-40.

In the case of Brendan, there is no secondary evidence from the Americas that he went anywhere. The only possible interest is that his stories exist at least in legend, and they parallel others such as the Greek story about the land of the satyrs. Taken together, it appears either that somebody had been sailing around the New World rather early or that several writers had vivid and parallel imaginations.

Other stories do exist but with perhaps even less evidence. Norse sagas tell the story of the Irishman Ari Marson who was driven by storms across the Atlantic in A.D. 983 to a land where he was baptized by Christians who had preceded him. But no other evidence exists for his journey, although one can speculate whether the Norsemen might have had any ulterior motives for writing the story.[7] Most of the tales, wherever they come from, point to a route west, into the Caribbean and Gulf of Mexico, as a logical end of a European voyage.

[7] Pohl, 261, for a summary of this voyage.

A prince is said to have made that voyage five hundred years after Brendan — on about the same amount of evidence. The man was a Welshman, Madoc (Madog) ab Owain Gwynedd, and in A.D. 1170 he may have found what was to become North America. For years, a mild controversy has been maintained as to whether Madoc sailed to America and perhaps the Gulf of Mexico in the twelfth century.[8] There is some evidence that he may have done so, or at least tried.[9] There is no evidence that allows proof.

Madoc was apparently a real Welshman but perhaps never a prince, although called so in later days. Madoc was a son of Owain Gwynedd (Owen Gwyneth), a Prince of North Wales, in an indeterminate line of succession. His father had numerous children, including many sons, whom even historians despair of unraveling but simply note that he "left behind him manie children gotten by diverse women. . . ."[10] These children (more than twenty) naturally quarreled over the succession, and

[8] Other early English explorations or claims of early explorations include the ships of Thomas Croft to North America in 1481 (Quinn, 278) and the better-known John Cabot in 1497 and 1498 (Hartwig, 335). These, however early and interesting, have nothing to do with the Gulf of Mexico and Caribbean area exploration. See also Eden's *The first Three English books on America*.
[9] Deacon, *passim*.
[10] Powel, 226 (see Powel, 193f).

Madoc thought it best to leave the land "in contention betwixt his brethren" and go elsewhere by "sailing West."

Whatever the original story, like St. Brendan's, it became considerably embroidered as the centuries went by. Perhaps unfortunately for Madoc and his reputation, the story was seized upon by both over-zealous Welsh chauvinists and Welsh detractors. Madoc became a legendary figure around whom revolved a collection of stories related to voyages west, most sounding a little too much like the imaginings of a poet.

Robert Southey—taking his background information from the bard Iolo Morganwg (Edward Williams, 1740-1826), who apparently made up most of his Madoc material, and Dr. Owen-Pughe, who did stick to probable fact amidst a host of inaccurate, romantic references—took Madoc not only to the Americas but also into an Aztec sacrifice. Madoc happily escaped, but his reputation has been damaged ever since.[11]

That there are some records attesting to a voyage of some sort is well known. Madoc, after a family dispute, made a voyage of exploration to an unknown land and found it to his liking. He returned and collected a colony of Welsh, "such men and women as were desirous to live in quietness," and took them to the west across the sea.[12] Just where Madoc established this colony is what remains in dispute. That he did in fact leave Wales is not usually questioned.

In 1584 David Powel compiled and wrote his *Historie of Cambria*, which collected much Welsh history, including the Madoc stories. Powel, dealing with old manuscripts and verbal stories, noted that the "common people" were wont to augment rather than to diminish tall tales. This had happened to Madoc, but Powel's opinion of Madoc's presence in the west was that "sure it is, that there he was."[13] Powel found few details of the voyage, but he notes that Madoc journeyed far south of Ireland and—in two voyages—settled a land that was later part of New Spain or Florida. Powel's opinion was that the Welshman went to "some part of Mexico."[14]

There are later writers who believe Madoc's voyage, but they have found no other evidence than had Powel. Their belief is not additional evidence. Richard Hakluyt, in his *Principall Navigations*, expressed his theory that Madoc had sailed at least to the West Indies or some other part of New Spain.[15] He does note that there may have been elements of Christianity in Indian beliefs before the Spanish arrived.[16]

Many of those who later remarked on Madoc's story also thought that the Gulf of Mexico was perhaps the end of the voyage or voyages. Part of the claim of Sir George Peckham, in

[11] Southey, *Madoc,* or Fitzgerald, ed. In Fitzgerald's edition, the work runs a turgid one hundred forty-eight pages.

[12] Powel, 222f.

[13] Powel, 228.

[14] Powel, 229.

[15] Hakluyt picked up his entry almost entirely from Powel, but changed the "Mexico" reference, for some reason, to "West Indies."

[16] Hakluyt, in the "Third and Last Volume" of the *Principall Navigations,* 133-35 in the convenient Glasgow edition of 1904.

his efforts to prove that England had an inherent right to much of the Americas, was that Madoc had sailed to the lands later called New Spain. Sir George may have had motives somewhat different from other historians.

Nevertheless, in this century the Daughters of the American Revolution placed a marker at Mobile Bay, Alabama, as the place of Madoc's landing. The marker depends not so much on older references to the voyage, perhaps, as on the fact that there may have been Welsh-speaking Indians north of there at one time. This unlikely occurrence has a long background and involves an Englishman who may have walked across Texas more than four hundred years ago.

David Ingram was an English sailor who, along with one hundred fourteen others, was set ashore north of Tampico in 1568. Ingram had been with a fleet headed by Captain John Hawkins, who was trading but also teaching Francis Drake about

Sir John Hawkins

the profits of pirating against the Spanish. Drake, later Sir Francis, learned well, but that is a different story.

Their small fleet of six English ships had stopped in Africa for slaves to help increase the profits of the trip, and all had gone well at first. The cargo had been illegally sold to the Spanish in the New World at a handsome profit, and the English had turned their attention to what Spanish ships they might plunder. Theirs was a curious business.

Caught by a sudden storm, the English fleet had little choice but to seek refuge in the Spanish port of Veracruz.[17] Their bad luck was just starting, for an unexpected Spanish fleet trapped them there. Four of the English ships were sunk, and two man-

The defeat of the British under Sir John Hawkins at San Juan de Ulloa

aged to escape. Francis Drake sailed the *Judith* out of the harbor and back to England as fast as he could. Hawkins's ship, the *Minion,* had taken on board most of the survivors from the other ships and, although it managed to escape the harbor, was so crowded that the men realized a run for England was impossible. "They very well sawe, that . . . if they perished not by drowning, yet hunger would force them in the ende to eate one another."[18]

That the English would not consider. More than a hundred men elected to take their chances ashore. Many walked back south to be captured by the Spanish; the rest went north. Only three of the latter survived, David Ingram, Richard Browne, and Richard Twide. They walked across Texas and on to the Atlantic and were eventually picked up by a French ship and returned to England.

David Ingram published his account, one of the first descriptions of the New World for English readers, some years

[17] If all this sounds unlikely, it was. The English traded with the Spanish (illegally, of course) as well as making their ships the subject of plunder. However, any port in a storm, as the old saying goes, was occasionally true. Actually, the English were not entirely seeking refuge. Hawkins notes that they had three hostage ships and passengers which they planned to exchange for food and time to make repairs. It was nevertheless a brave and somewhat reckless move. Trouble developed after the arrival of the Spanish fleet, and a fight started later.

[18] Miles Philips in Hakluyt's *Principall Navigations.*

later in Hakluyt's collection of voyages. Of note were his remarks concerning the use of Welsh by native American Indians. One bird, similar to a goose, had received a name curiously like "penguin," which to Ingram "seemeth to be a Welsh name." "And they have," Ingram continued, "also in use divers other Welsh words, a matter worthy the noting."[19]

Indeed, such a thing was worth noting, and people did so for the next three hundred years. Sir Walter Raleigh made the same such observation,[20] followed by many others. One of the clearest reports in later years was that of Governor John Sevier of Tennessee about an Indian chief who recalled stories of the Welsh arrival in America (and a landing near Mobile Bay) and of traders who spoke Welsh with various groups of American Indians. The stories were common through the end of the nineteenth century.[21]

A great amount of information was eventually gathered to support the fact that some Indians of North America, perhaps the Mandans, were of Welsh descent and spoke a form of Welsh.[22] A number of people attested that this was so, but no recordings were made, no transcripts were gathered by trained linguists in the field, and the language — if it ever was used in America among Indians — does not exist today.

The evidence for Ingram's walk, and Hawkins's voyage itself, is rarely questioned now, even though the main documentary difference between it and Madoc's presumed voyage is a small collection of secondary documents: a corroborating comment by Spanish and English government records. It was so questionable for a time — at least Ingram's part of it — that the narrative was removed from a later edition of Hakluyt.

Whether New Spain or Mexico or somewhere else in North America was the end of Madoc's voyage — or whether it actually happened — will probably never be known. There is simply not enough evidence to constitute proof.

The only fact that exists is the legend itself. Madoc's questionable return from somewhere, after an initial voyage of exploration, with stories of a land across the sea, did become legend in Europe. By all accounts, at least, he never returned from his second voyage. Whether his adventures became legend in the Americas as well is not clear. There were early stories among some North American Indians about a group of people coming from the east over the sea, but the stories have apparently died out. The Aztecs had the legend of Quetzalcoatl, a white man who came from the east. It was because of this legend (and a great number of Indian allies) that Cortés found the conquest of Mexico at first relatively easy. Zealous supporters of Madoc

[19] Hakluyt, *Principall Navigations*, 560.

[20] Deacon, 66.

[21] Deacon gives a collection of the stories, as well as a fine outline of the controversy. See also the collected documents by Burden which do support the existence of spoken Welsh among American Indians in the eighteenth century.

[22] Deacon, 207f.

see the adventurous Welshman in the stories of this Quetzalcoatl; detractors see only coincidence in the stories of a white man arriving from the east into the Gulf of Mexico . . .

Which proves that legends are hard to prove.

The Relation of Dauid Ingram of Barking, in the Countie of Essex Sayler, of sundry things which he with others did see, in traueiling by land from the most Northerly partes of the Baie of Mexico (where he with many others were set on shoare by Master Hawkins) through a great part of America, vntill he came within fistie leagues or there abouts of Cape Britton.

 'Bout the beginning of October, Anno 1568. Dauid Ingram with the rest of his company being 100. persons in all, were set on land by M. Iohn Hawkins, about sixe Leagues to the West of the riuer La mina, or Rio de Minas, which standeth about 140. leagues west & by North from the cape of Florida, who trauelling towards cape Britton, spent about 11. moneths in the whole, And about seuen moneths thereof in those Countries, which lie towards the North of the riuer of May, in which time (as the said Ingram thinketh) he traueiled by land two thousand miles at the least, and neuer continued in any one place aboue three or foure dayes, sauing onely at the Citie of Balma, where he stayed sixe or seuen dayes.

Kings. There are in those partes (sayth he) very many Kings, commonly within a hundreth or a hundreth and twenty miles one from an other, who are at continual warres together: The first King that they came before, dwelt in a Countrey called Giricka, who caused them to be stripped naked, and wondring greatly at the whitenes of their skins, let them depart without further harme.

Large precious stones. The Kings in those Countries are clothed with painted or colloured garments, and thereby you may know them, and they weare great precious stones, which commonly are Rubies, being 4. inches long, and two inches broad. And if the same bee taken from them, either by force or sleight, they are presently depriued of their kingdomes.

The Kings in their maiestie. When they meane to speake with any person publikely, they are alwaies carried by men in a sumptuous chaire of Siluer or Christal garnished with diuers sortes of precious stones.

The maner of saluting their kings. And if you will speake with the king at your first approching neere to him, you must kneele downe on both your knees, and then arise againe and come somewhat neerer him, within your length, the kneele downe againe as you did before. Then take of the earth or grasse betweene both your hands, kissing the backside of each of them, and put the earth or grasse on the crowne of your head, and so come, & kisse the kings feete. Which circumstances being perfourmed, you may then arise and stand vp, and talke with him.

How to know the noble men. The Noble men and such as be in special fauour with the King, do commonly weare feathers in the haire of their heads for the most part, of a Bypde, as bigge as a goose of russet colour. And this is the best marke that this Ingram can giue to know him by.

Pearle. There is in some of those Countries great aboundance of pearle, for in euery cottage he found pearle, in some houses a quart, in some a pottle, in some a pecke, more or lesse, where he did see some as great as a beane. And Richard Browne one of his companions, found one of these great pearles in one of their Canoes or boats, which pearle he gaue to Mounster Campain, who tooke them aboard his ship, and brought them to Newhauen in France,

The initial page of Ingram's account showing the ambiguity of the place of landing. "Florida" included Texas at the time. The distance in leagues northwest is (perhaps) incorrect, the distance traveled east is (perhaps) correct, to place the landing in the western Gulf of Mexico.

Map of Scandinavia

THE VIKINGS IN WARM WATER

he Vikings were a people to generate legends. Accounts and artifacts support the fact of their travels from the Mediterranean to Central Russia and from Greenland to Africa.[1] Further west than Greenland, the stories are thin. The Norsemen are, however, strong contenders as the European discoverers of America—or at least one-time discoverers whose discovery was not too successful. Their western claim rests on a number of sagas, stories written centuries after the actions they describe; one or two archaeological sites; a few questionable New World artifacts; church records; and a collection of runes on rocks. There are no original maps. Early Vikings apparently did not have time for maps.[2]

Few people today doubt the truth of Viking voyages in the north Atlantic, including that of Bjarni Herjulfson who apparently saw North America in A.D. 986 after he was blown there while trying to reach Greenland.[3] He did not land. Bjarni was on his way, with great resolution, to join his father for yuletide ale and could not be persuaded to go ashore, even though his crew gave him "hard words" about his refusal to land.

Greenland had been settled by Norse and native Icelanders around A.D. 950. Erik the Red was foremost of these settlers, and it was his son Leif who, apparently curious, reversed Bjarni's route and sailed to Vinland about 1000.[4]

[1] Jones, for the best general history.

[2] For a close translation of the early sagas, see Anderson's *The Flatey Book*. On later charts, see Kohl. See Pohl, 238f, for the questionable North American artifacts and 299 for a Norse chronology. Wallace, 155f, gives evidence that the North American artifacts are not authentic.

[3] Or A.D. 987 or 985. See Taylor, 253; Mowat, 873.

[4] Bruun, Mowat, *passim;* Pohl, 276f.

After Leif came Thorwald, Thorfinn Karlsefni, and his wife Gudrid as part of a colonial effort. The Karlsefni's son Snorri was born near or in Vinland about 1007. These settlers were followed by other Norse whose ultimately unsuccessful colonies beyond Greenland came to an end as late as 1360 and probably much before.[5]

Greenland and Vinland even had their own series of bishops. Quite a few were duly appointed by Roman officials over some two hundred years, the first being Erik Uppsi (Gnupsson) in 1112.[6] Even before such church records began, before the sagas were written down, Adam of Bremen mentioned Vinland in 1073, the earliest dated reference that has survived. But where was Vinland and the other places the sagas mention west of Greenland? How far did the western voyager go?

This is not exactly known. Most scholars think Vinland was someplace on the northeast American coast.[7] Speculation on other possible sites strays into sheer guesswork. Dr. Helge Ingstad has discovered remains of Norse settlement at L'Anse aux Meadows, Newfoundland, which most professional archaeologists term clear, reliable evidence. The controversy of Minnesota's Kensington runestone is perhaps not settled, but a mere handful of people think it genuine. Then, there are only a few investigators—and perhaps no professional archaeologists—who believe various islands in the Caribbean, the coast of Mexico, and sites in Paraguay were visited and settled by Viking groups.[8]

Imaginary concept of the discovery of Greenland by the Norse

Viking boats could sail any part of the north Atlantic. They were sixty to a hundred feet long, up to twenty feet in beam, could be beached easily, and were also excellent river craft. They

5 The sagas are available today in many translations such as the admirable Penguin series, but see *The Flatey Book* for facsimiles of the Flatey manuscript, the Hauksbook, the *Saga of Erik the Red,* and the Vatican manuscripts; Mallery, 60f.; Jones, 255; and Mowat, *passim.*

6 Bolton, *Terra Nova,* 46; Ingstad, 88; Schmidt, 276, 283.

7 Bolton, *Terra Nova,* 33, gives a good summary; see also Pohl, 308, for a list of Vinland localities, according to about fifty authorities, ranging from Greenland itself to Florida.

8 Pistilli, Holland, Pohl, Bruun, Fischer, and Jones.

sailed best before the wind, could be rowed fairly well by a crew of from six to thirty men, but were at the mercy of adverse storms.[9] They were capable of coasting North America and traveling on many an inland river.

But capability says nothing about an actual visit. If the Vikings ever sailed the warm waters of the Gulf, their journey is now preserved only in legend. Juan de Torquemada does record an Indian story of such a landing — very close to Pánuco. He says that Mexican Indians met people from northern regions — white, fair-haired, bearded, finely built — who arrived wearing clothes of dark sacking, open in front, without cowls, cut out round at the neck, with short, wide sleeves. The dress fits that of northern Europe, or the Norse Greenland settlements, after A.D. 1000.[10]

These newcomers, traveling south and inland, were welcomed as they passed through the area of Tollan and settled for a time near present Cholula. This, of course, is an origin — one of several origins — of the Quetzalcoatl story. Those who came, in ships that looked like serpents and whose sides were girt with an ornament of coiled snakes, later departed saying that others would come again.

At least it is a story that the Spaniards had no motive for inventing. Concerned with colonial claims, the Spanish were usually reluctant to admit precedence.

If Vikings saw present Texas, it was on this trip down the coast from the decks of their ships. The clearest evidence of a very different nature attesting to a Viking visit in the Texas area comes from a site in southeastern Oklahoma, in the drainage of the Red River. A state park on Poteau Mountain near Heavener houses the much-studied, eight-character runic inscription called everything from a fake to the coded evidence of a Norse visit on St. Martin's Day, November 11, 1012.[11]

ᚠᚢᛞᚠᚱᚲᚷᛈᚺᛏᛁᛇ
ᚲᛋᚤᛖᛏᛒᛗᚨᛁ ᛜᚹᛝ

Runes from a Norse futhark

Certainly the date is logical. A monk, traveling with the group, would have been capable of writing an encoded message — and his presence, as a Christian, was an accepted thing among Vikings of that year. This is exactly the opinion of some contemporary scholars who claim that the stone, and several others found

[9] Tornöe gives a mariner's estimate of the ships, saying that a square-rigged vessel could sail two hundred miles a day and operate at fair angles into the wind.

[10] One source for the rewritten story is Herrmann, 165f.

[11] Landsverk, Farley, *passim.* See also Pohl, *Atlantic,* 45f. Wyckoff, state archaeologist for Oklahoma in 1971, gives facts on both sides and states his conclusion that Viking presence in Oklahoma is "premature and unjustified" as a finding.

[12] Long, *passim,* quotes an Oklahoma City man, Lester Shipley, who said he carved most of the stones about 1937. He did not do the Heavener stone (although he said he saw someone working on it), which was observed much earlier. See Farley, *passim.*

[13] Then there is the ephemeral story of the "Viking Boot" discovered in Montague County—a semifossilized boot with a leg and heel bone protuding from within. (McGee, *Runestones,* 65-66.) Whether it is Norse, or even a boot, has not been determined.

[14] See Krause, 71, 74; cf. Kirkland, 84, 141, 152.

[15] Whipple, 37-38; Kirkland, 205. The observer noted that the series of paintings containing the ship were "dim, and many of the details obliterated, giving room for Imagination to fill up the details to her own satisfaction."

[16] Richardson, referring to Cleng Peerson, and in fact relating him to Erik the Red, called "the first Norse immigration agent for America," 1. The memories persist.

nearby, are all the work of not-too-transient Vikings in the early eleventh century.

The controversy continues. Unquestionably genuine runic engravings in the New World are simply unheard of. They gain no acceptance from the majority of American or European scholars. Indeed, at least one person has come forward to claim he carved some of the Oklahoma stones, but other first-hand observation dates the carving long before his lifetime.[12]

On Texas rocks, no definite runes—fake or otherwise—have come to light, although there are fleeting stories about carvings in the Panhandle and along the Rio Grande.[13] Perhaps the trouble in Texas is that there is little suitable rock (the Vikings especially liked granites and well-cemented sandstones) on coastal landing sites.

Some rock engravings of what seem to be Norse ships appear in Europe, and at least remotely similar outlines are found painted at Texas sites in Seminole Canyon on the Pecos, Blue Mountain in Winkler County, and at the Paint Rock site in Concho County.[14] But to call these representations Norse ships (done perhaps by Indians) within hearing of most Texas archaeologists is to risk instant ridicule. And justified ridicule it is, because of the very weak argument supporting the "Norse ship" claims.

Some images have even faded away. At the Rocky Dell site, in Oldham County in the Texas Panhandle, a government surveying party reported seeing a rock painting resembling a ship with sails.[15] It is rather an unlikely place for sailing craft. In any case, the copies made at the time are now lost, and the original has been effaced.

The present-day Scandinavian Texans, at least the Norse of Bosque County and the Danes in the colony of Danevang, look with pride to their ancestors. The Viking blood, as the Danes say, "is still warm in our veins," and the Norse sport such headlines as "When the Norsemen Came to Texas: After Eight Centuries a Mild-Mannered Carpenter Leads His Race to New Homes in Land Discovered by Viking Ancestors."[16] As far as "first arrivals" go, some of the Scandinavians insist they simply never stopped arriving. Whether or not they were actually preceded by settlers arriving in longboats is simply—at present— not known.

There are those who believe that historical fact should be displayed as exact scientific fact or not at all. There are those who believe that speculation is instructive. And there are those who think it pleasant that not everything is positively known. Perhaps some questions should never have answers.

"It may be fitting that the legends of the Northmen should . . . supply just that indistinct and vague element which is needed for picturesqueness."[17] At any rate, the legends are still around, some of them valuable because they provide examples of ways of thought.

[17] Anon., "Visit of the Vikings," 515.

Shore parties of de Gama's crew gathering food

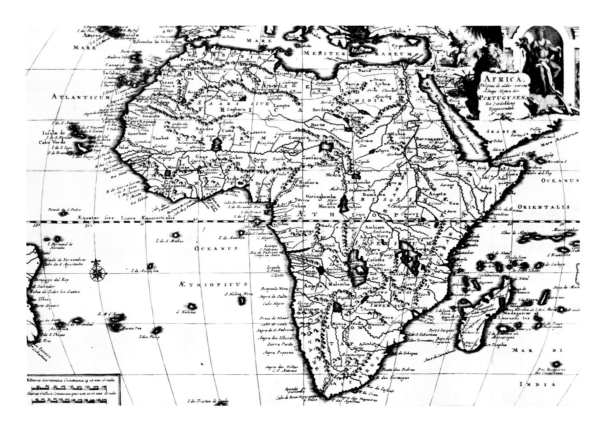

AFRICAN SAILORS AND
A LOST COLONY

Legends of the Vikings are well known. Not so well known are the stories of African explorers and traders which parallel those told of the Norsemen — and on as grand a scale. In A.D. 1311 Abubakari the Second, ruler of Mali, stood on an African shore, overlooking the surf, and stared westward. Before him lay a great mysterious sea. He had been told that either strange lands or the end of the world lay on the other side. Behind him stretched the kingdom of Mali, as large as Europe and more powerful.[1]

Abubakari had been assured by learned men from Timbuktu's university and by Arab geographers that the world was indeed round and that new lands lay on the other side of the great green ocean.[2] At least one geographer, Abulfeda, at the turn of the thirteenth century, spoke of possible voyages around the earth.[3] Still, there were those who said that the sea bordered the end of the world. Abubakari, tiring of petty wars and even the trade of gold to Europe, decided to find out.

The price was high. Earlier, he had assembled enough troops, craftsmen, and supplies on the west coast to build four hundred ships, half solely for supply, to cross the ocean. The ships were of all types and sizes; Abubakari took no chances.

[1] Van Sertima, *passim.* Chapter 3 of Van Sertima's book is his narrative treatment of Abubakari's story. But the dates and even the name of the ruler are in question. The best reference (Al 'Omari) does not give the name of the mariner king and does not connect the name of Abubakari with a voyage. The mariner is known as Kankan Musa's predecessor (Davidson, 74). This section is based on Van Sertima's book to some degree but directly on Al 'Omari's *Masalik Al-Absar;* Hennig, *Eines Neger-Sultans, passim;* and Davidson, 73-75, 89-95.

The medieval Mali kingdom, largely Moslem in faith, is best known for the ruler after "Abubakari," one Mansa Musa who took the throne sometime between A.D. 1307 and 1311.

There is considerable division of opinion about the actual year (Davidson, 90 f, *Encyclopaedia Britannica* V: 22, 70).

The kingdom itself, a Mandingo state known as Melle or Mali, was traditionally founded in 1213, almost two centuries after the Almoravid (reform Moslem) expansions south had brought the Moslem faith and trade to trans-Sahara Africa.

The initial date of the university at Timbuktu is not known, but it existed throughout much of the Mali kingdom. Its existence, and the existence of many learned men in town, gives rise to a curiosity. Timbuktu, of course, was a crossing place of spectacular trade goods. European glass and sword blades, North African copper and salt moved south; while slaves, beautiful or strong, and hundreds of pounds of gold moved north. In spite of this, Leo Africans curiously noted that the trade in manuscript books was more profitable than any other business (Davidson, 93).

Africans wrote a couple of centuries after the founding of Songhay—the next kingdom. Whether he meant profit in terms of unit profit or absolute value is not known, but conditions were about the same under Mali kings.

The importance of this learned trade was direct upon the history of the New World. It is probable that any geographical knowledge of the New World that had been gained by African sailors might have come to the attention of people in Spain or Portugal (Davidson, 72f). The hints of the coasts of the New World and Gulf of Mexico that appear on some European maps before any known European

The fleet sailed, and the year revolved slowly. Only one ship came back, that of a timid captain who had turned around just as the other ships were caught by a powerful westward-flowing current which had been expected. The captain had no news other than that he had seen the rest of the ships sail on west.

Obsessed with thoughts of the western ocean, Abubakari would try again. Around him now lay the second effort: a similar fleet paid for with the gold of his empire and the toil of thousands of subjects. Ready were his best seamen and navigators, captains and cooks. The ships this time also would carry colonists and trade goods—just in case—and one ship had a throne elevated on the deck, covered by a royal parasol.[4] Abubakari would lead the second voyage himself. A drummer would stand nearby so the words of the king could be sent from ship to ship.

When all preparations were made, Abubakari handed over the government to his brother and departed. The ships were soon surrounded by a horizon of water. Abubakari and his fleet never returned to Africa.

Where Mali's ruler landed is unknown today, but there is some evidence that he finally arrived in the New World, possibly on the western shores of the Gulf of Mexico, and settled with hundreds of followers.

The city of Timbuktu, as known to the English in 1830

Some evidence, that is. The departure of the fleet is perhaps conclusively certain, but where it went is not, although a few reviewers of the data already write in terms that assume the case is proven.[5]

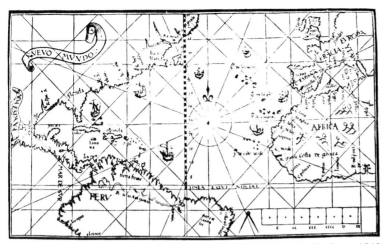

Map from Medina's, Arte de Navigar, *1545*

Perhaps full records of these Atlantic voyages still lie hidden in Arabic literature. If so, they may someday come to light. Many known works by earlier Arab geographers simply speak of the Atlantic as the green ocean that marks the end of the world. The Chinese, however, with one of the more complete historical records in existence, preserve stories of the great ships which sailed west from Africa to a land of strange trade goods. They apparently had heard of such voyages in the course of their trade with India and Africa.

What two Chinese geographers, Chou Ch'u-fei and Chao Ju-kua, write sounds plausible. Chao, writing his Chu Fan Chi, the Record of Foreign Peoples, about A.D. 1226, and quoting from Chou, speaks of a land called Mu-lan-p'i:

> To the west of Ta-shih, there is a sea, and to the west of this sea there are countless countries, but Mu-lan-p'i is the one visited by the big ships of Ta-shih. Putting to sea from T'o-pan-ti in Ta-shih, after sailing west for a full hundred days, one reaches this country. A single one of these ships carries a thousand men and on board they have stores of wine and provisions as well as weaving looms. When speaking of big ships, there are none as large as those of Mu-lan-p'i.
>
> The products of this country are extraordinary; the grains of wheat are two inches long, the melons six feet around—enough for a meal for twenty or thirty men. The pomegranates weigh five catties, the peaches two catties, citrons over twenty, . . .[6] Rice and wheat are kept in silos for tens of years without spoiling.

sailors visited there may be shadows of Arabic manuscripts that were taken to Spain by the Moslems. Since the Spanish were efficient in burning Arabic manuscripts after the expulsion of the Moors, all traces of this connection may be destroyed. As a sad example, Cardinal Ximenes destroyed some eighty-four thousand Arab documents in the public squares of Granada (Jeffreys, *Pre-Columbian,* 26).

[2] See, however, the opinion of Al-Masudi who, although knowing the shape of the earth before A.D. 956, thought that the Green Sea of Darkness was impossible to navigate (Bovill, 61, and Hennig, "Arabische 'Abenteurer,' " *passim*).

[3] Davidson, 74. See also Jeffreys [Jeffreis] in *Scientia,* 207.

[4] Al 'Omari, 69.

[5] Robinson, 16. The author follows the usual "It has been proven beyond all doubt . . ." and "This remarkable information has been known for a number of years by the close inner circle of archaeologists and anthropologists who have been very reluctant to divulge it." See Cole, *passim.*

[6] The cattie is a unit of weight of about one and a half pounds.

[7] An alternate, plausible reading is given by Li, 115, who suggests (after Dr. Lien-sheng Yang) that the reference could be to the increasing length of a sundial shadow.

[8] Mostly from Hirth and Rockhill, 142-43; and Li, 114-15; with author's changes.

[9] Hirth and Rockhill, *passim.*

[10] Li, 115.

[11] Li has made the only earlier guesses, 123.

If one travels by land further two hundred days journey, the days are only six hours long.[7] In autumn, if the west wind arises, men and beasts must drink at once to keep alive. If they are not quick enough about it, they die of thirst.[8]

Often dismissed as fiction,[9] this account can be easily interpreted as a fairly accurate description of a land across the Atlantic from the Old World.[10]

The natural products, however strange they sound, can be tentatively identified.[11] The grain of wheat could be an ear of early American corn, unfamiliar to the Chinese and worth

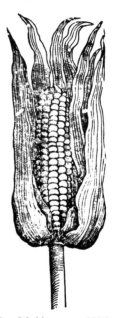

New World corn, c. 1606

mentioning whether they had seen it or merely had a description from an Arab traveler. The melon might be a pumpkin; and the pomegranate, peach, and citron could be the soursop or sweetsop, the avocado or papaya, or the pineapple. Yet the primary question is where Mu-lan-p'i and T'o-pan-ti are or what the Chinese meant by the terms.

The name Ta-shih (however tempting to claim this is a Chinese transcription of Tarshish) was apparently applied by the Chinese to the Mohammedan world.[12] Present-day Morocco and part of the Iberian peninsula would be included. Neither Ta-shih nor T'o-pan-ti can apply to something in the eastern Mediterranean, because a trip across the width of that inland sea would not be described as a hundred-day voyage in open water to a far land of strange products. The Chinese knew the Mediter-

[12] Li, 116; Hirth and Rockhill, 119.

ranean in the thirteenth century and also knew of the west coasts of Africa and Spain. The home port of these great ships probably was on the Atlantic coasts of North Africa or southwestern Spain.

Whatever place the name Mu-lan-p'i referred to, ships that went there were commented on even earlier, in the fifth century, in China.[13] That the ships existed, and at such a size, is attested to by several writers.[14] Chou Ch'u-fei (K'u-fei) not only discussed ships of the Indian Ocean but also the larger ones on a Western Sea beyond the Arab countries.

[13] Li, 121, speaking of the Shu-i-chi attributed to Jen Fang (A.D. 460-508).
[14] Hirth, 27-34; Davidson, 181f.

Nineteenth century engraving of Chinese ship at Singapore

The ships which sail the Southern Sea . . . are like houses. When their sails are spread they are like great clouds of the sky. . . . A single ship carries several hundred men. It has stored on board a year's supply of grain.[15]

Chou notes that the ships sailing the Indian Ocean contain all that is necessary for crew and passengers for a long time. Once the voyages are undertaken, he says, the ships do not stop for anything, not even someone's death. These are certainly not coasting vessels, for the shallows are the only dangers they fear. When under way, nothing can be seen from the ships except the ocean, until landmarks are sighted.[16]

Yet ships of the Western Sea, Chou relates, were the biggest of all. One could carry a thousand men and had marketplaces aboard. These huge ships were capable of a voyage of years if winds were unfavorable.[17]

[15] Li, 117; Hirth, 33-34.

[16] Hirth, 27; and the narrative of Fa-Hsien.

[17] Li, 117.

[18] Hirth, 28-29. But see Beazley, I: 490, who claims the Chinese used the compass in the third century A.D. Another speculation is that the compass was known in the first century A.D. (Hirth, 28). South was, often, the primary orientation for Chinese maps and compasses.

[19] Quatrefages, 200-202.

[20] Martyr, III: 1; Wiener, II: 13; Wright, 325. See also Galvano (Galvão), 48, for accounts of the "curled haire" of these New World blacks.

[21] F. Gomara, LXII; Wiener, II: 13.

[22] Wiener's opinion, *passim*.

[23] Wright, 326.

[24] Wright, 329.

[25] Wright, 328. Blacks assisted in the building of the first European vessel on the American coast with Lucas Vásquez de Ayllón's colony in Virginia and with Vasco Balboa on the Pacific in 1513.

[26] Quatrefages, 199-201.

Exaggeration, happily, appears to be more common in early Chinese records than pure fabrication.

Navigation, as far as the trips described in these documents are concerned, was carried out by sailors before A.D. 1000 through observation of the sun and moon or by knowledge of prevailing winds. Not until the twelfth century was the compass in use aboard Oriental ships. It was usually just a magnetized needle—the "south-pointing, floating needle."[18]

But the stories of these great ships now rest on the authority of just a few writers, who, after all, may have been elaborating upon stories they heard after too many glasses of wine. One needs other kinds of evidence to decide whether these or other voyages actually took place. There is little.

Blacks—from somewhere—did apparently precede the Spanish to the mainland New World. At least Spanish explorers spoke of them. The reports mention groups of black men isolated or living with native Indians, perhaps the fragments of a former colony or the survivors of an earlier shipwreck.[19]

Peter Martyr, a historian and contemporary of Columbus, notes that Spanish explorers found "Negro slaves" in Darien, present Panama, who were fierce and cruel.[20] "It is thought," the chronicler observed, "that Negro pirates of Ethiopia established themselves after the wreck of their ships in these mountains."

These Africans, for that is what Martyr means by his use of "Ethiopia," were individual captives of local Indians (not slaves in the later sense, but captives of war) and had apparently come from a nearby colony. They were there before 1513 when Balboa found them.[21]

The explanation that they were former pirates is probably invented. That they were actually there probably was not. That they might have been African traders, perhaps shipwrecked years before, is at least possible.[22]

It is more likely that this group, and others noted in the Gulf area, might have been escaped Spanish slaves. The first were brought to the West Indies by the Spanish about 1501.[23] Not only the blacks who came with the Spanish as free men but also many slaves were certainly independent-minded people capable of taking care of themselves in a new world. Whether shipwrecked explorers and traders or later slaves, the Africans were not always the people pictured in the usual cliché: stone-age tribesmen taken from a jungle. There were those in the New World who could write beautiful Arabic,[24] those who were shipbuilders, and others possessing a host of professions.[25]

The Spanish in their first explorations around the Gulf of Mexico noticed a sprinkling of black colonies.[26] The one in

Texas was seen relatively late, and hence it cannot be dated early enough for a claim to be made that it was anything other than a group of escaped slaves from the Caribbean or Mexico.[27]

It was on the lower stretches of the Rio Grande, in a place within the present city of Brownsville, that the first of the Spanish colonizers and explorers reported a group of blacks.[28]

[27] Hill, 50, 78.

[28] Hill, 50.

Fanciful meeting of explorers and Indians

Captain Carlos Cantú, who had earlier led a group of Spanish colonists northeast from Nuevo Leon in 1749, came across a colony of blacks on a river island in the braided lower Rio Grande.[29] Speculation on the origin of the people, noted as being independent and well armed, was wide ranging. They were called escapees from earlier slave ships or stranded mariners or were simply left unexplained, like the blacks seen in present-day Panama before Balboa. That they preceded the Spanish to the mainland is well known, but whether they preceded the Spanish slave trade to the New World is not known. The Texas colony, apparently quite durable, was identifiable until the nineteenth century. However, few scholars today believe the colony was pre-Columbian. In any case, the colony disappeared rather suddenly before the 1830's, perhaps as the result of a disastrous flood. By the turn of the century, all that was left in the way of evidence were ghosts, some say, and mysterious fires seen late at night that leave no ashes to be blown by the morning's wind.[30]

[29] Hill, 78-79.

[30] Benavides, *passim.*

But there is an earlier type of evidence concerning the western Gulf of Mexico. What exists is a mixed body of material evidence, very limited in scope. In the Mexican civilization called Olmec a number of stone heads exist as possible evidence of a visit or colonization scheme originating in Africa. The colossal

[31] Van Sertima, von Wuthenau, *passim.*

[32] See von Wuthenau, *passim,* e.g. *Unexpected Faces,* xv, 18-21. Von Wuthenau also includes examples of European and Levantine physiognomies, e.g. *Art* includes a charming "Phoenician" bride, 180.

[33] E.g. Jeffreys, *Scientia* article, 231, which is a misreading of Hooton.
[34] Hooton, 168, 181, 183; Jeffreys, 213.

[35] Flores, 14.

[36] Schwerin, 8-9.

[37] Schwerin, 18f.

heads have the faces of African blacks, and they dominate Olmec remains. Far too old to be connected with Abubakari's voyages, they appear to be realistic portraits of blacks who could have come not as slaves or mercenaries, but as explorers or traders. There is perhaps no other known motive for such sculpture, and the great hewn blocks are certainly not fictional.[31] Whether the faces are portraits or not is a viewer's judgment. The faces also match many a contemporary Mexican face. One can ask, therefore, where the facial characteristics came from? The large Olmec heads and other figurines from later centuries seem to represent African racial types with startling accuracy. [32] But this is not proof that the sculptured faces are portraits of Africans who came to the western Gulf. They do present an ethnic facial structure that exactly resembles contemporary African faces from the Mandingo-Mali area. But they may only attest to coincidence.

No evidence such as huge rock heads comes from within Texas's present boundaries. The often-cited "Pseudo-Negroid" human skulls mentioned by Earnest Albert Hooton are not applicable.[33] Some writers have taken his look at materials from the Pecos Pueblo in New Mexico to refer to Texas.[34] Some skulls were examined in New Mexico which were close in measurements to "Negro groups" of Africa but by no means identifiably so. They were not statistically close to measurements of other Indian skulls in the area but well within skull variations for any ethnic group.

Normal variations in skulls and other skeletal remains are enough to make questionable any racial conclusion based on one or two examples. Most authorities on Mesoamerican Indians consider that the question, definition, and determination of "race" cannot be applied. In particular, "attempts to establish differences based on . . . characteristics such as . . . form of the cranium (or anything else) yield no consistent classifications."[35]

Other evidence than carved heads or skulls is necessary, therefore, before one can even begin to consider whether early African voyages are "true." Contemporary efforts have used evidence from plants—agricultural and domesticated crops—that could have been brought to the New World or taken to the Old.

A few cultivated plant species, the bottle gourd, jack bean, and one variety of cotton, almost certainly were transported or spread naturally from the Old World, usually meaning Africa.[36] Probably only the gourd could have simply drifted across an ocean by itself. Cottonseed, valued as a source of oil and food long before the fiber-bearing varieties were artificially selected by man, could not survive an ocean drift.[37]

Yet the dates for the arrival of these plants in the New World are, according to present estimates, too early to be connected with any known human voyages. The bottle gourd reached northeastern Mexico as early as 7000 B.C., and cotton by 1000 B.C.[38]

Other food plants are often said to provide proof of early Atlantic crossings. Yams *(Dioscorea)* may have been in the West Indies before Columbus and, if so, were brought from Africa;[39] the taro *(Colocasia)* is also apparently an African plant brought to the New World.[40] Going the other way, the manihot root and maize are found in Africa and have been attributed to Portuguese importation after 1500. But the Portuguese themselves made no such claims, and the crops were too extensive in Africa by the early 1500's to have been started only a few years before.[41]

Another popular source of evidence is languages — rather, the similarities between them. Evidence of linguistic similarity is one of the least satisfactory forms of evidence in the minds of almost everyone except its defenders. To Leo Wiener,[42] it is clear that native African languages left an indelible mark in the native Indian languages of the New World long before Spanish or other European voyages. In addition, Wiener sees other Mandingo cultural influences in Mexican civilization. In a thousand pages, he compares Mexican Indian civilization with Mandingo and concludes that the two are not just similar but "identical, in concept, in form, in ritualistic observances."[43]

On largely linguistic evidence,[44] Wiener dates the arrival of Mandingo merchants in the New World to the first quarter of the fifteenth century. This kind of contact, if it happened and if it happened early enough, could have resulted in the creation of the black god of traveling merchants seen in the few surviving Mexican Indian codices.[45] Or the color could be ceremonial or accidental. Claims and speculation are not proof.

Wiener's claims are very wide. He cites similarities between African and New World Indian cultures concerning the shield design of Aztec warriors (reflecting the crescent design in Africa),[46] sacrificial practices,[47] the costuming of the gods,[48] the structure of worship,[49] calendar similarities,[50] and artistic motifs. According to Wiener, Arabic-African talismanic designs, called *gadwal,* occur also in the Americas in a wide band from Mexico to Tennessee. The recurrent motif is a square, often with looped ends, at times enclosing a cross and embellished with symbols.[51] Whether such detail represents proof of influence or chance is in the mind of the beholder. After such an array of what Wiener believes is evidence, there is no doubt in *his* mind, at least: "The matter of chance is mathematically excluded. If chance can play

[38] Schwerin, 4, 5, 27.

[39] Schwerin, 23, thinks that more work is necessary at the species level before this can even be claimed.

[40] Jeffreys, 214.

[41] Jeffreys, 216; Wiener, III: 359, 369.

[42] Wiener, *passim.*

[43] Wiener, III: xi.

[44] Wiener uses Sahagún as a primary reference, working from the French edition of 1880: *Histoire générale des choses de la Nouvelle-Espagne* (much from Book IX).

[45] Wiener, III: 257.

[46] Wiener, III: 237-38.
[47] Wiener, III: 249.
[48] Wiener, III: 260f.
[49] Wiener, III: 296f.
[50] Wiener, III: 298.

[51] Wiener, III: 268f; Holmes's *Art in Shell,* 286f.

such pranks, then all historical, archaeological, and philological conclusions are null and void. . . ."

Written evidence is rarer still. North African evidence (not necessarily black African) of early arrivals in the Americas is claimed by Barry Fell, who theorizes pre-Columbian North African exploration and active settlement in North America. Fell has been reading the Great Basin curvilinear Indian pictographs, long an enigma to American archaeologists, as early Arabic.[52] He has interpreted many shield-like rock paintings as copies of Mediterranean coins. He has, however, received little support for his claims from American archaeologists.[53]

As far as local evidence goes, the Texas area itself seems to remain a crossroads. One of the most curious stories concerns legends from the Mexican Indians themselves — possibly the most reliable source — attesting to ancestors coming down the Texas coast. But, because of the destruction of Mexican Indian records largely during the Spanish conquest, the legends are filtered through Spanish voices.

According to Bernardino de Sahagún, the ancestors of the Mexican Indians came by sea from the east and north. They traveled, he understood his Indian informants to say, from the direction of Florida, around the curve of the Gulf of Mexico to the Pánuco area (about as far west as they could sail).[54] They

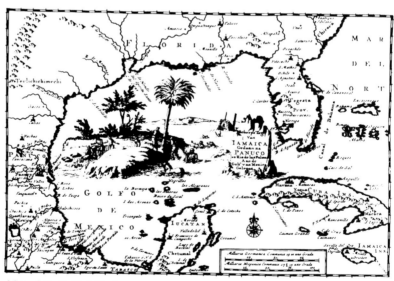

Map of the Gulf of Mexico

came looking for an earthly paradise, a new home. And they came in seven ships.

Various people have used this voyage, with little other evidence, as proof that the Indians of Mexico were influenced

[52] Fell, *Saga America,* 248, 314f.

[53] Cole, *passim.* In fact, some professional archaeologists simply call Fell a "looney."

[54] Sahagún, *passim;* Jairazbhoy, 8.

by the northeast Africans—the Egyptians.[55] Similarities in ritual, concept of existence after death, artistic motifs, forms of the deities, athletic costume, all have been cited in support of Egyptian influence (and racial mixture) with Olmecs, Mayans, and Aztecs.[56] There are indications that Rameses III (1195-1164 B.C.) did send out ships on expeditions, even into the ocean of inverted water.[57] And in his tomb an expedition of seven departing ships is painted.[58] His explorers may have sailed the Texas coast, but none apparently returned to Egypt.

The Mayan *Popul Vuh* states that such ancestral arrivals—unfortunately it does not specify where they came from—were a mixed bunch, black and white, who came far from the east—down the present Texas coast. But there are no details. The Spanish destroyed Mexican Indian literature with such zeal that the full story, true or false, is probably destroyed for all time.

What is left admits varied interpretation. And it may be that one occasionally sees only that for which he searches.

[55] Jairazbhoy, *passim*.

[56] Jairazbhoy, for instance.

[57] Jairazbhoy, 13; Breasted, 1906-7, IV: 203.
[58] Jairazbhoy, 15.

The lands discovered by Columbus, from the illustrated letter to Gabriel Sánchez, Basel, 1493

ONE OF THAT COMPANY OF EXPLORERS

In 1500 the New World did not exist—at least not in most European minds. Something was west of Europe, across the Atlantic Ocean, but it was not a new world. Christopher Columbus had sailed three times to a strange-looking collection of islands and a questionable mainland, and he stoutly maintained that he had reached Asia. To be sure, however, he had seen only the easternmost edge, peopled with bright birds and savages. He had not seen the sprawling cities and markets Marco Polo had visited by going the other way, but that it was Asia could not be in doubt.

At first there was no new world and there were no new names such as Caribbean or Mexico or America. The first maps, showing "part of Asia" and other such words on their western edge, were kept jealously as royal secrets. The log books and diaries of the first explorers, including those of Columbus, were confiscated or "borrowed" by kings, never to be seen again.

The first maps were splendid guesses considering what was known. Many people—most navigators and scientists and humanists and whoever would believe them—knew that the earth was round. That had been known, off and on, for two thousand years before Columbus's voyages.

Although various legends existed about Atlantic or Pacific crossings, there were few stories about ordinary people circumnavigating the globe. Not many people had thought about it, much less considered if anything might be in the way. Yet to a few it seemed logical that one could reach Asia by sailing west, but the journey seemed so much more risky than going east — until political conditions made the eastern passage almost impossible. But no one knew how far west one had to go. The earlier, reasonably accurate measurement had been lost. Columbus, however, thought Asia was quite close and finally convinced the rulers of emerging Spain to finance a trip.

Christopher Columbus

The stories Columbus told on his return were delightful and confusing. What he reported of the part of Asia he had seen — when he was not talking about an earthly paradise — did not seem much like the India or China that Europeans knew about.[1] The bronzed people Columbus brought back were called Indians, sure enough, but they fit no known description of Asians. To make matters worse, some of the sailors and pilots who sailed with Columbus did not support his stories. They swore, under Columbus's glittering eye, that they had been to Asia's mainland, but privately they denied their oath.[2]

Ferdinand of Aragon and Isabella of Castile, actually the rulers of Spain, decided to check on things. A few years after Columbus's initial voyage they turned to a person who apparently

[1] Arciniegas, 154; Parry, *The Age of Reconnaissance;* Sauer, Part I.

[2] La Cosa, on his return, mapped Cuba as an island, not the mainland of Asia. Jane, 222; Gould, 2; Oldham, "The Importance," 101. Columbus may have

would be an objective observer, a person who could accompany a voyage of exploration as a reporter, not as a man of conquest and not as a person who would personally benefit from the trip. They chose a Florentine merchant living in Spain at that time, Amerigo Vespucci.[3]

Engraving of Amerigo Vespucci

This Florentine, by a curious chain of events, would become perhaps the first European known by name to sail the coast of Texas as well as to have his name applied to the lands of a new hemisphere.[4] The naming was a chance act by a young cartographer who did not personally know Vespucci, but exploring what was to become known as the New World was not chance. Vespucci would be the one to popularize the concept that across the Atlantic was not Asia but a new land—the New World.[5]

Southern Europe, by the late fifteenth century, was a hotbed of activity: political, scientific, artistic, and mercantile. The century held in many ways the creation of worldwide trade and banking. It was the century of the Renaissance and the creation of art as we know it today. These were the years of Leonardo da Vinci and Botticelli,[6] of the Medici, of the growth of modern political nations, and the establishment of the power of the church in governments as well as in the minds of men. It was the creation—but for some scientific theories—of the modern world.

And it was a world based largely on fact—empirical fact—that could be checked and proven. Ferdinand and Isabella,

thought, however, that a new continent lay to the south of his most northwesterly reaches. He said that the coast of South America was a mainland, and one unknown till then—if Las Casas's transcription is to be believed *(Historia,* II: 264). However, he was only placing the "earthly paradise" in a land to the south and still believed Asia to be just to the northwest (Castañeda, *Our Catholic Heritage,* I: 1).

[3] The general controversy over whether Amerigo made any voyages, or some voyages, is a splendid example of historical inquiry. And feelings run high (see the Washburn review of Arciniegas in 1956 and the most humorous statement in Zweig, 101). The tone of this chapter itself would have been grounds for academic argument—and quite possibly *ad hominem* attack—not too long ago. Ranged generally on the side of Vespucci, or at least neutral and still in the minority, are Angelo Maria Bandini, Francisco Adolpho de Varnhagen, Henry Harrisse, John Fiske, and Germán Arciniegas, among others. Vespucci's chief detractors are Las Casas, Antonio de Herrera, Fernández de Navarrete, Baron Humbolt, Viscount Santarem, Duarte Leite, Alberto Magnaghi, and Frederick Pohl, to name a few, although most of these writers agree with some of the voyages, but not if they detract from Columbus's first attaining the mainland. Most texts today cite Piñeda as the first European to sail the Texas coast, even when mentioning the possibility of Vespucci or other unnamed voyagers. What is perhaps the best statement is that the fact of Vespucci's voyages—in particular the first—cannot, at present, be proven nor disproven—unless one believes the few early maps that exist both show the Gulf of Mexico and were based on Amerigo's reports.

[4] Amerigo's grandfather bore the name, which may come from

Amalaric (Arciniegas, 3). It is not a saint's name, so the infant, upon baptism, was called Amerigo Mateo. The Mateo was soon dropped. Vespucci comes from *vespa*, wasp, used on the family coat of arms. After Vespucci settled in Spain he was commonly known as Amerigo.

5 Arciniegas, 226-27; Zweig, 38. Amerigo was not the first to use the term Mundus Novus. Even Columbus once had told the Spanish sovereigns that they had another world, and Peter Martyr used the terms Nova Terrarum, Novo Orbis, from 1493 — but Columbus clung to the idea that the land was Asia nevertheless, and the earlier references were more honorary than literal. Amerigo made the term refer literally to a new, unknown land, and his letters popularized the idea. Vespucci letters, Ann Arbor, 88.

6 Botticelli painted most of the Vespucci family, including young Amerigo.

7 Vespucci was born on our March 9, 1454, but very near the end of the Florentine year 1453; Pohl, 207; Arciniegas, 3. For his life, see Pohl and Arciniegas.

8 Arciniegas, chaps. IV, VIII.

9 Arciniegas, chap. XI.

hearing Columbus's stories and the stories of other less publicized voyagers, sent out an expedition in 1497 to confirm reports of the land beyond the sea.

Vespucci was then forty-three years old.[7] He had been educated in the scientific and humanistic traditions of Florence and had served both as businessman and political agent for the Medici.[8] He counted as friends many of the politicians, artists, geographers, and scientists of the day. To Spain he had originally come as an agent investigating Florentine investment, but he stayed to become a businessman in his own right.[9] Opportunities were obviously greater in what must have seemed a frontier country to Vespucci.

He became known as an outfitter of ships and a cosmographer, a dependable businessman and a convivial conversationalist — talents he had acquired in Florence. He was, apparently, more of a humanist than a man after quick honor or profit and was thus a good choice as reporter to the king.

Sailing as a pilot or navigator, Vespucci left Cadiz in May of 1497. However knowledgeable Vespucci was and however directly in the service of a king, he led neither this voyage nor

Contemporary artist's concept of Amerigo Vespucci off the Texas coast, c. 1497-1498

10 Guesses have included Vicente Yáñez Pinzón, Juan Díaz de Solís, and Juan de la Cosa. At the time it probably did not matter. Arciniegas, 160.

11 Vespucci letters, preface, Ann Arbor, 87.

any other expedition, and the names of the captains have been lost.[10] Very much in the spirit of the time, or at least for those voyages he was on, Vespucci describes himself as simply "one of that company of explorers."[11]

Sailing southwest, the expedition stocked final provisions in the Canary Islands, then crossed the Atlantic with favorable winds.[12] The ships, four in all, sailed through the islands discovered by Columbus, across the Caribbean, and made landfall at 16° north latitude.

Vespucci was later to become one of the foremost cosmographers of his day, appointed Pilot Major of Spain some years later, his job to certify maps and navigational equipment for Spanish voyages. He even calculated longitude at least once with remarkable precision in an age when longitude was routinely considered impossible to calculate directly.[13] On this voyage he missed the longitude by about 5°.[14] But latitude was easier. With the quadrants of the day he could figure his angular distance from the equator within an error of about half of a degree. On a coast tending north and south, a half-degree error in latitude could mean a thirty-mile difference, but at latitude 16°N in the Caribbean, with east-west coasts at that location, he could have landed in present-day Belize, Guatamala, or Honduras.[15]

Allegorical engraving of Vespucci the explorer

Wherever Vespucci first saw the continent, from that point on, he was entranced. Of course, it was easy to be entranced. His voyage was not one of conquest. These explorers were not charged with finding piles of gold and spices, great cities or eastern potentates. They were to observe and report on what they actually saw. The voyage was therefore the earliest known scientific voyage, or humanistic venture, or pure exploration to the New World. This feeling of entrancement shows in Vespucci's letters. His book on the voyages, naturally given to the king, naturally disappeared. But some of his letters remain.

[12] Presumably. The trip was twenty-seven days in duration if the right figure has been preserved in manuscript. Pohl, 26; Arciniegas, chap. XI; Vespucci's letters, Ann Arbor, 89. See also Arciniegas, chap. XIII; Lowery, 125f.

[13] Pohl, 118-19; Arciniegas, 192f.

[14] And at other times missed completely, as when he said he had been 150° from the meridian of Alexandria. Yet, if the remark has been preserved without error, it is a strange one: "I was 150° from the meridian of Alexandria, which is eight hours from the equatorial hour." Alexandria is eight hours (120°) east of the Gulf of Mexico, the westernmost Amerigo may have been, but not 150° west.

[15] Apparently the most serious technical objection to the first voyage is suggested by Roukema, who applies the figures of traverse tables ("diff. lat." sailing) to rather colloquial remarks in letters intended for general readers— the implication being the routes were simply traced off a map. (See also Harrisse, 357.) In Roukema's article Vespucci advocates are simply "hopelessly bedazzled." The article does point out that the "torrid zone" ends at the first climate (12° 45′ N) and the second climate's boundary is confused. The interpretation of Vespucci's first voyage as an impossible, or fictional, voyage taken from other accounts is based on taking the directions in the letter as actual sailing instructions, which they were probably not meant to be. Roukema, *passim;* see also Levillier, *passim;* and Batalha-Reis, 197f, on the evaluation of data in general for the period.

Allegorical engraving showing Vespucci "disembarking in the New World." The background shows the often-illustrated cannibal account; the foreground shows Vespucci, astrolabe in hand, confronting "America" in her hammock.

Reaching a green and, compared to European standards, a primitive land, Vespucci summarizes his first landfall:

> Here we dropped the bow anchors and stationed our fleet a league and a half from shore. We then lowered a few boats, and, filling them with armed men, we pulled as far as the land. The moment we approached, we rejoiced not a little to see hordes of naked people running along the shore. Indeed, all those whom we saw going about naked seemed also to be exceedingly astonished at us, I suppose because they noticed we wore clothing.[16]

Vespucci, unlike some explorers, was always able to recognize the viewpoint of the people he met and realize the shortcomings of his own culture:

> I suppose we should have learned much more,
> had we been able to understand their language.

The voyage moved north and west, apparently circling Yucatán and coasting the Gulf of Mexico.[17]

> The land is very rich in birds, which are so numerous and so large, and have plumes of such different kinds and colors that to see and describe them fills us with wonder. The climate, moreover, is very temperate and the land fertile, full of immense forests and groves, which are always green, for the leaves never fall. The fruits are countless and entirely different from ours. The land itself is situated in the torrid zone, on the edge of the second climate, precisely on the parallel which marks the

[16] Quotations are from the Ann Arbor edition of *Cosmographiae Introductio,* translated by Joseph Fischer and Franz von Wieser — an edition that should be read in full. (See pp. 90, 102, 112-13 for the subsequent quotations.) The entire account gives Vespucci's feelings as well as the first impressions of this land. As a humanist reporter, Vespucci not only gives a favorable impression of the lands of the New World but also records pleasant and unpleasant encounters with the natives. He frankly titillates his readers with accounts of the unbridled sexual practices of the natives and describes how he and others (at least on one occasion) were most generously offered women for the night. He pointed out that the women were graceful and beauti-

tropic of Cancer, where the Pole rises twenty-three degrees above the horizon.

Vespucci gives no specific description that can be linked exactly to that part of the coast which is present-day Texas. Perhaps he had less to say, because from offshore the Texas coast is not greatly spectacular or interesting, if one likes lush tropical forests and geographical relief. Later voyagers called the Gulf coasts low, barren, and inhospitable.[18]

Padre Island near Point Isabel, August 25, 1924

Vespucci's letters are always those of an explorer, not a conqueror. And he is not above humor:

> . . . when they [the natives] asked us whence we came, we answered that we had descended from heaven to pay the earth a visit, a statement which was believed on all sides.

The first voyage continued for eight hundred seventy leagues, found little evidence of gold, took thirteen months to complete, and collected much data.[19] Peaceful contacts as well as battles between the sailors and the natives took place. The expedition took a few prisoners and products of the new land and sailed for home.

Vespucci was to make other voyages to the new continents. His reports, including comments on cannibalism, hammocks, and geography, gave rise to some of the first European impressions of the New World. Vespucci had a talent which almost brought his reputation to ruin (though not during his lifetime) and placed his accomplishments in academic doubt: He was a good writer.

Columbus's reports of his voyages did not stir the imagination. For one thing, most of Columbus's words were kept secret or, along with his journals, officially lost. For another,

ful of body, and naked, and "showed a great desire to have carnal knowledge of us Christians" (Arciniegas, 169). He includes brutal tales of cannibalism which influenced European engravings of American Indians for generations *(Mostra Vespucciana,* Tav. XII, XIV). He describes iguanas, hammocks, warfare, bathing, and almost endless wonders to catch the reader's attention. Some of the warfare between sailors and natives may have been fictional. At the time, it was illegal to take slaves unless they were captured in war. Vespucci makes it clear that this was done, except when he makes it equally clear that natives volunteered to return to Europe. Both certainly could have happened and did on many a voyage to the New World.

[17] Valentini, 299. A curious point, however, is that Valentini, although accepting Vespucci's voyages, assumes Vespucci gave the data of the first voyage to the Portuguese while sailing for the Spanish. Vespucci did, on later voyages, sail for the Portuguese. Apparently there were no hard feelings in his lifetime, for he was Pilot Major for Spain until his death. The map Valentini considers, of course, might not be Portuguese.

[18] Harrisse, 167-68.

[19] Harrisse, 354. Any exact estimate of the league is impossible. The distance would be at least over eighteen hundred miles.

Supposed first European woodcut of American Indians, c. 1505

20 Although he waited several years, well after his official reports to the court. He wrote most often to Lorenzo di Pier Francesco de'Medici and Piero Soderini. After becoming a Spanish citizen and Pilot Major, Vespucci never again wrote to Florence (Arciniegas, 282).

21 Zweig, 32, 75.

Columbus did not correspond extensively with anyone other than his king and queen. Vespucci did.[20] He was reared in a humanistic tradition where one composed essays or poetry, painted pictures or church murals, and sang in state programs and to one's love in the evening. He had been taught that in life one was expected to perform, to report, to be an artist in the Greek meaning of the word poet — to be a maker. Vespucci wrote letters to his former Italian friends, and these friends quickly made the letters public.

They were as popular in Europe — in many translations — as newspapers are today. In fact, they were the newspapers of the day.[21] Vespucci, like any good writer of the time, blended personal speculation and fact, travel notes and scientific observations, and laced this with enough local color, sex, atrocities, and honest poetical beauty to catch anyone's attention.

And Vespucci knew full well that the land he had seen was not Asia. He said that what he had seen was a new world, unknown to the ancients and wreathed with the mystery and challenge of the unknown. And here, Vespucci touched on a constant, common feeling in the minds of most later arrivals to the places that would receive strange-sounding names like Venezuela, Mexico, and Texas.

Vespucci's letters, circulating in Europe in a handful of "editions" and languages, created a great interest and an equally great controversy.

In 1507 a small group of scholars — printers, geographers, poets — gathered at Saint-Dié, Lorraine, for the purpose of publishing learned works under the sponsorship of the Duke of Lorraine, René II.[22] It was not an unusual venture considering

22 Zweig, chap. 4; Arciniegas, chap. XXII.

the spirit of the day and new and potent inventions such as the printing press. Here, in April, the young priest and geographer Martin Waldseemüller, or the vicar and writer Jean Basin, or the poet Matthias Ringmann decided that "America" would be a good name for those lands across the Atlantic. Basin or Ringmann christened the land America in the production *Cosmographiae Introductio*, intended to update the geographical concepts of the day in the light of the new transatlantic discoveries, and Waldseemüller put the name on his huge world map issued at the same time (on the South American section).

The group almost certainly did not know Amerigo Vespucci personally, and they certainly knew about Columbus — as well as perhaps other voyages across the Atlantic — but Vespucci's letters carried the day. Copies of his letters were altered to fit their work and published as part of the *Cosmographiae Introductio*. One of Vespucci's originals was addressed to the Gonfalonier Piero Soderini of Florence, a friend. Vespucci's comments to Soderini were altered, simply by a name switch, to refer to René — and therefore rendered ludicrous. The personal references, left in, do not fit. But at the time, what reader would know? Further, copyright laws were unheard of in 1507. And such was the power of the printed (or engraved) word — and perhaps such was the obvious parallel between Asia, Africa, America — that the name stuck.

And the name stuck much to the disgust of later "Columbians." Some years after Vespucci's death, various writers decided that Amerigo had deliberately usurped the fame of Columbus and contrived to have the continents named after himself — and had in fact been on no voyages at all. Amerigo was then and since called a "lucky imposter," a "fatuous personage," and a "lying novelist." Ralph Waldo Emerson considered it "strange . . . that broad America must wear the name of a thief . . . the pickle-dealer at Seville."

Where did this side of the story start? Is there truth in such allegations? Is it of more than idle curiosity to know whether the man whose name was given to the New World continents might also have been the first European known by name to sail Texas waters? Or did he sail at all?

Father Bartolomé de Las Casas was the first to raise his voice against Vespucci, apparently through a desire to defend Columbus. He gave no reason or documentary proof for his charges that Vespucci was a usurper of fame not deservedly his. Las Casas, the sixteenth century defender of the American Indian and attacker of the brutal type of conquistador, took on Vespucci as an object of denigration. To Las Casas, Amerigo was a man

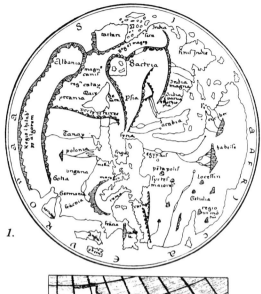

1.

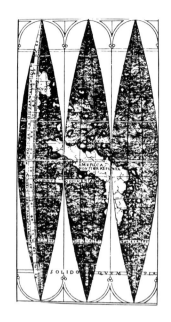

2.

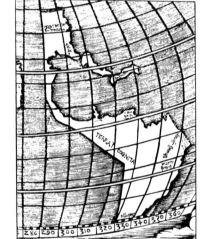

3.

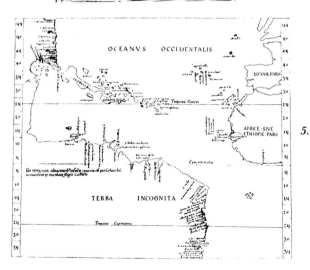

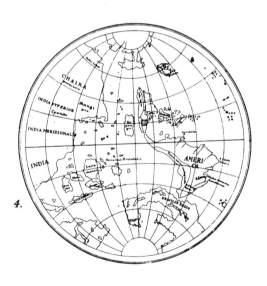

4.

5.

1. *A world map by Petrus Vesconte, c. 1320*
2. *Lodavicus Boulenger's map of America, 1514*
3. *Map of North and South America after Ptolemy, 1512*
4. *Drawing of Johann Schöner's globe of 1515*
5. *Tabula Terrae Nova from a 1513 edition of Ptolemy*

of questionable liberal thought and a convenient scapegoat for the way Columbus had been officially treated.[23] That Columbus and Vespucci had been friends—as shown by their correspondence—was ignored.[24] If Las Casas had any proof for his opinion, he did not print it. Vespucci's contemporaries apparently accepted his voyages as genuine and believed in the truth of his reports.[25]

But Las Casas's opinion was not forgotten. As it became clear to later writers just how badly Columbus had been treated by Spain in return for his brilliant discovery, Amerigo apparently became an easy object of blame. Because copies of Amerigo's letters had been translated and retranslated by others, they could easily be questioned as to their authenticity.[26] The originals are lost. Amerigo's full manuscript which he called "The Four Voyages" was given to the king—and kept or lost.[27] Very few official maps, unfortunately not including the master map kept by the Spanish government, now exist. It was surprisingly easy—years later—to charge that Vespucci made only two voyages, or only one, or none.[28]

Columbus's maps and journals likewise disappeared. Las Casas's rewriting of Columbus's diary does exist but did not become an object of scrutiny as did Vespucci's letters.

No fact, however, exists to contradict any of Vespucci's voyages, and most indications are that he could have made them.[29] And no remarks by Columbus or Columbus's sons indicate that Vespucci was suspected of having usurped anything due Columbus. They do indicate a friendship.

[23] Arciniegas, 259f; Zweig, 79.

[24] Arciniegas, 159. Columbus's letters to his son Diego prove he was hoping for aid from Vespucci. Arciniegas, 258; Zweig, 98.

[25] Harrisse, 353f.

[26] Pohl, 149f. They may have been changed also for political reasons. Arciniegas, 222-23.

[27] Arciniegas, 235.

[28] See Batalha-Reis, 198f, on the danger of drawing conclusions from silence or a lack of documents; Zweig, 92.

[29] Harrisse, 354-55.

Exploration . . . a large part of childhood (or adulthood) play . . . a "cartoon" from 1875

[30] *Mostra Vespucciana,* 73f; Lowery, 129; and the fine short article by Dixon, "Maps and the Discovery of Texas."

[31] Arciniegas, 161; Dixon, "Texas History in Maps," 5.

[32] Arciniegas, 160, quoting López de Gomara *(Historia general de las Indias,* chap. liii), who says that many set out to the new-found lands, some at their own expense, but as most made no immediate gain, no recollection of them remains; Harrisse, 360-61; Lowery, 130.

[33] "Almost all the historians of geographical discoveries consider it their absolute duty to arrive at a radical conclusion in the study of problematical questions, answering with a *yes* what only deserves a *perhaps,* or, more frequently, dismissing with a *no* what ought to be held as probable." Batalha-Reis, 210. See also Oldham, *passim.*

The maps that exist are ambiguous. There are several before 1515 which show what may be the Gulf of Mexico, but their interpretation depends a great deal upon the opinion of the observer.[30] That there was a continuous coastline to the west of Cuba, that it was concave to the Caribbean and Atlantic, was certainly known.[31] But that there were other voyages than Amerigo's to bring reports to Europe before 1510 is certainly true. The officially recorded trips, the voyages of exploration known today, are probably the minority.[32]

In any case, Amerigo Vespucci is a strong contender for the title of the first European, known by name, to sail the Texas coast.[33] And if he did, he sailed it strictly in the name of exploration, not conquest.

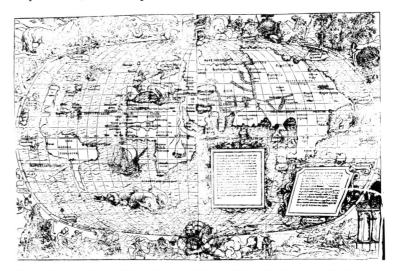

Typus Cosmographicus Universalis, from Novus Orbis Regionum, *edited by Simon Grynæus, 1555 edition, frontispiece*

FILLING IN THE MAP

In the summer of 1519 Alonso de Piñeda, sailing for Francisco de Garay, the Governor of Jamaica, took a fleet of four ships east to west around the Gulf Coast.[1] His voyage was not just exploration; it was a voyage to secure the land northwest of the Gulf of Mexico against the possible expansion of Cortés.[2] Limits to the New World, limits to exploration, were already realized, and Spanish conquistadores and governors scrambled for claims amid a cloud of royal documents of permission and military moves.[3]

Piñeda's voyage allegedly was made also to check on the remote possibility that a strait, not discovered but already named the Strait of Anian, existed from the northwest Gulf to the Pacific. At least it was an excuse, for maps showed a disturbingly solid continent. It was becoming clear that the Spanish could not sail straight through to the western sea and the Orient.[4]

The land in their way, however, would yield natural products, much silver and a little gold, and prove a valuable colonial holding for some three hundred years.

Piñeda's voyage produced an excellent sketch map of the Gulf of Mexico—it did not establish incontestable claims.[5] Garay sent another expedition the next year, under Diego de Camargo, to start a colony. This effort was definitely not a voyage of exploration. It included a hundred and fifty men, seven horse-

[1] Piñeda's name may really have been spelled Pineda, Pinedo, or Piñedo, and he may have only had three ships; but there is fair agreement on most of his route. He was off the Texas coast most probably in June and July of 1519. Castañeda, I: 1-3, 6-11; Lowery, 149-53; Farmer, *passim;* Harrisse, 163-73 (citing Bernal Diaz).

[2] Castañeda, I: 13f.

[3] "Permission" could be royal or could be authorized from delegated governing bodies such as the Priors of the Order of the Hieronymites (Harrisse, 166).

[4] See Lowery, 123-71, for a good summary of the exploration of the Gulf coast, particularly east of Texas.

[5] Often called the first to depict the Texas coast, and probably done by Antón de Alaminos, the only known person to have all the map's data at his command (Farmer, 111).

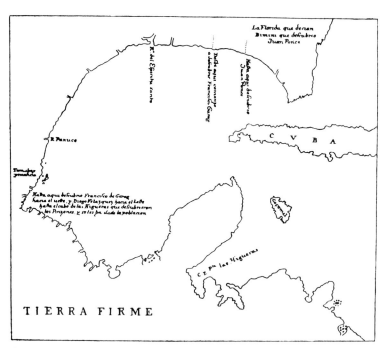

Copy of Piñeda's map of the Gulf of Mexico

[6] There has always been contention whether the Rio de las Palmas spoken of in this period was the Rio Grande. Most distances from known places indicate that it was. Castañeda affirms it is from his sources (I: 11-25). Lowery says no in his text (153), but in his notes also cites references which indicate the river was at 26°30' N which is within about thirty miles of today's Rio Grande.

[7] Castañeda, I: 21f; see also above note.

men, artillery, and bricks and lime to build a fortress. They almost certainly tried to establish themselves at the Rio Grande.[6] But they failed. Earlier, the Indians had made Piñeda welcome but had not so received Camargo. They proved quite warlike and inflicted a defeat on the Spanish shortly after their arrival. Probably as the result of a misunderstanding or because the Spanish became bothersome if not outright abusive, the Indians attacked first on land, then—after the Spanish had taken refuge in their ships—by canoe. The Spanish were driven into the sea, and Camargo eventually joined Cortés.

Garay, however, refused to give up, even though the future Texas area was becoming a problem, and many of the men he sent out simply joined his rival, Cortés. In June of 1523 Garay himself, armed with a royal grant, sailed not as an explorer but as a colonizer to found the first town in the new area. The sixteen-ship fleet arrived at the Rio de las Palmas, probably the Rio Grande, on July 25, 1523.[7]

Garay brought the first European provisional government, a city council, to the future Texas area. The town was named Garay, and Alonso de Mendoza and Hernando de Figueroa were "elected" alcaldes—all this before they arrived. In a way, this was the first town government in the present area of the United States, but it was unsuccessful. It is not even certain whether the "town" was ever established on land.

The area then was not known as Texas. Under Garay it was called Amichel and was known later as La Provincia del Río de Pánuco e Victoria Garayana. It was not a part of New Spain, which was a formal name for regions south of the Pánuco.[8]

Once landed, Garay sent Gonzalo de Ocampo in late July to explore upriver. He may have gone as far as present Brownsville, but he did not like the land. Perhaps his report was really execrative, but for some reason, Garay decided to move on south to the Pánuco River, or beyond, and to confront Cortés. The expedition traveled south and overland. The king, however, had just reconfirmed Cortés's rights to the Pánuco area, and Garay was essentially defeated both on land and on paper.

[8] Most of the time . . . for a short time, New Spain extended to the Rio de las Palmas, under Cortés's rule. This was quickly countermanded by the king and the new province of Garayana created.

Cortés, conqueror of Mexico

Many of Garay's men declined to follow any farther so unfortunate a conquistador and openly opted for Cortés. Garay decided to journey on to Mexico where he was hosted well by Cortés—since he represented no threat. Garay died just after Christmas Day. Cortés said he died of a broken heart, the doctors said of pneumonia, and others said of poison.[9]

Garay was formally succeeded in 1525 as governor of the lands between the Rio Grande and Florida by Nuño de Guzmán. Guzmán maintained his reputation as one of the most brutal conquistadores, setting up slaving near the Pánuco, decimating native populations, and voiding earlier land grants.

[9] Castañeda, I: 28 (Cortés, *Cuarta Carta de Relación,* October 15, 1524, in Barcia, *Historiadores Primitivos,* I: 129-65).

Copy of codex drawing showing a battle of the Spanish conquistadores in Mexico

[10] Castañeda, I: 36.

Guzmán did launch an expedition into the Texas area, under a very inexperienced cousin, Sancho de Caniedo.[10] This effort crossed the Rio Grande, exploring an unknown distance north, but by this time Pánfilo de Narváez had been appointed governor of the Rio de las Palmas area and therefore of future Texas lands. Shifting governors and royal permissions were more confusing for would-be conquerors than coastlines were for the explorers. Caniedo went north in 1528. His five-month expedition was a failure in terms of any accomplishment and was remembered only for hardships. Hostile Indians, insects, marshes, a lack of supplies, and probably poor planning dictated a return south.

It remained for other overland Spanish explorers to fill in the map of future Texas. They were plentiful enough for an area that provided no rich mines and was in large part quite unpleasant to walk across.

Álvar Núñez Cabeza de Vaca, Estéban, Andrés Dorantes de Carrança, and Alonzo del Castillo Maldonado crossed Texas in 1534-1536 as survivors of the doomed expedition Narváez had captained. They had been Indian captives near the coast since their shipwreck in 1528 and only count as accidental explorers. Others fully intended to explore the new land. Francisco Vásquez de Coronado crossed the high plains, no one

Title page of Álvar Núñez's Relacion, *1542*

knows where for sure, in 1541. Luis de Moscoso de Alvarado, leading what was left of De Soto's expedition, saw much of northeast Texas the next year. Antonio de Espejo crossed the trans-Pecos in 1582-1583, and Gaspar Castaño de Sosa explored the mid-Rio Grande and the Pecos River in 1590.[11] These, among half a dozen other overland explorers—all after the 1520's— essentially, but very generally, defined the area.[12]

Journeys of exploration now became journeys of settlement, missionary activity, and colonial effort including the establishment of local governments.

The land bordering the northwest Gulf of Mexico, the land soon to be commonly known as Texas, would eventually be a buffer zone between holdings and incursions of French, English, and Anglo settlers. Through this land area would run the northern line of Spanish presidios and missions but only light Spanish settlement. Such hopeful names as "The New Philippines" and even "Florida" would yield to Texas or Tejas, the two spellings used interchangeably.

When this happened, fully at the turn of the sixteenth century, exploration in the grand sense was over. The land could be explored in detail; the general outlines were known. Now the map could be filled in.

[11] See Skeels for a map showing many of the routes of exploration by century.

[12] Literature, in abundance, exists on explorers after 1520 in the Texas area. E.g.: Bolton's *Coronado;* Bolton, ed., *Spanish Exploration;* Horgan, *Conquistadores in North America;* Lummis, *The Spanish Pioneers* (includes Docampo, "the man who walked further on this continent than any other," 102); Hodge, ed., *Spanish Explorers* (splendid collection of narratives, like the Bolton ed. above); and Bancroft, *Works,* particularly the History of Mexico, vols. IX-XIV, and the History of the North Mexican States and Texas, vol. XV.

A ship at night

EXPLORATION

he stared out over the bluff which fell a hundred feet, then another hundred, cascading to a distant flood-plain. The sunset poured back into his eyes, golden and blinding, but far below he could see miles of silt-covered bottomland lush with grass and trees. Who would have guessed such a place existed in this flat, desert country? And where did the river come from? And did it flood in the spring? He counted the days. It was time to turn back. Now he needed to find the landing place of the ship that would pick him up. He thought that he could.

She carefully scraped a thin, even layer of soil away from the bottom of the exactly square hole in the earth. The Texas sun beat down, flat and hot. Mosquitoes droned in slowly from the marsh to the east. For every one killed, two more appeared. Sweat ran down the back of her neck, and she tried to work precisely in the shadow of her large hat. Then her trowel touched, very lightly, the edge of a human bone. She picked up a brush.

What was that he had seen in the inscription? The second group of strange characters in the line of writing almost certainly represented the king's name, Darius. The name was written  and almost certainly was said Daraya-vaush. This and other names gave further sounds and meanings for other unknown characters. 𒉺𒅈𒊓 was Parsiya, "Persia." The language could be read.[1]

[1] See Bermant, 82 (chap. 4) for comments on Rawlinson's work translating cuneiform. This paragraph does not attempt to reproduce the actual thought arriving at the present transcription of Darius's name.

Fanciful wood-engraving of Balboa discovering the Pacific

Exploration happens, of course, when one goes looking—looking for something new. A new place, a new idea, a new way of doing something. Not all explorations are successful, but then success is not necessarily measured by what one finds. The process itself may be worthwhile.

The explorer often is also the one who first interprets and judges what is found. His first impressions of a new world or a new idea may be responsible and accurate or irresponsible and false. He may be able to decide the truth of what he sees, or he may not. The explorer is the person who assembles evidence of what he has found and is usually the one to report on his finds.

Most sixteenth century exploration and discovery was not theoretical—it was a very practical operation. No one, in the great age of geographic discovery from 1450 to 1650, deliberately just went voyaging into nowhere or headed for the south pole. The explorers traveled in logical directions to places they supposed to be reasonably possible goals. Explorers usually have at least legends, myths, or good guesses to rely on—and usually more.

In the sixteenth century they sailed for practical reasons: gold and spices, slaves and land. At that time the "New World" just happened to be in the way.[2]

[2] Parry, *Discovery,* xii.

And, of course, the New World, any new world, is only new to the outside "discoverers." It well may be peopled by those who know it very well indeed. It may be settled. And that condition calls for conquest in addition to exploration — at least in the minds of sixteenth century Europeans.

It should be noted that there are clear differences between the explorer and the settler — at least in the geographic sense. The explorer goes for the first time into areas unknown to him. But he does not stay for any length of time. Or at least he does not intend to stay. One of his goals is later to describe to others how to go where he went — and if it was worth it. He is the sketcher of the first maps, the compiler of the first descriptions. He wants to know exactly where he is. Most explorations are backed by a large amount of organization and money, yet the task remains in spirit an individual job. And the explorer almost never travels with his family.

The settler, however, leaves to go to a place already generally known, and he does not expect to return. He is not a reporter. He expects to live elsewhere and is often a part of a family. Nor does the settler care exactly where he is. Boundaries of ownership may come to be a problem, but he is not charged with defining his location in relation to where he came from.

Columbus's fort of Navidad from the published letter to Gabriel Sánchez, Basel, 1493

Exploring, like settling, is often a physical activity. To many people it means going where no one has been before: climbing mountain ranges, crossing trackless deserts, or penetrating dense rain forests. But exploring can be part of decoding and translating a lost language, mathematically describing the way a star explodes, painting a portrait, investing money, falling in love, or dealing with kitchen leftovers.

Exploring can also include part of the activity of a child making new friends after his parents have moved to a strange town or an adult going into a library for the first time. Exploration has been described as a form of growth, the explaining of the universe in human terms, and one of the most fundamental of human activities.[3]

Exploring is more a state of mind than it is physical activity. It involves risk and change, innovative thinking and action. It depends a great deal on imagination and curiosity, and demands a flexible, independent turn of mind. It appears to be a fundamental capability of creative individuals as well as a source of excitement and joy.

Without the capacity for exploration — physical and mental — mankind would probably be, in the words of an old cliché, little more than a collection of apes.

[3] The source of this stolen sentence is largely from NASA's symposium (Cousins). The best comments therein are probably Captain Cousteau's. See also Andrews, for the classic, early-century attitude toward exploration: accept hardship (for the love and advancement of knowledge), admit no nonsense (except dry humor), perform no heroics (perhaps), and take along no women (absolutely).

Time changes all things, however.

Navigator using a cross-staff to sight the North Star

Chapter I

東山經

又南三百里曰獨山其上多金玉其下多美石末塗之水出焉而東
南流注于沔其中多鯈蝞 其狀如黃蛇魚翼出入有光見則其邑大旱

又南三百里曰泰山其上多玉其下多金有獸焉其狀如豚而有珠
名曰狪狪 其名自訆 環水出焉東流注于江其中多水玉

又南三百里曰北山錞于江無草木多瑤碧激水出焉而東南流
注于娶檀之水其中多茈蠃

Chapter IV

Xenophon, writing one of his dialogues, refers to the organization of the Phoenician sailors. His character Ischomachus used the observation, among other army and navy analogies, to encourage his wife to greater order around the house:

Once I had an opportunity of looking over the great Phoenician merchantman . . . and I thought I had never seen tackle so excellently and accurately arranged. For I never saw so many bits of stuff packed away separately in so small a receptacle. As you know, a ship needs a great quantity of wooden and corded implements when she comes into port or puts to sea, much rigging, as it is called, when she sails, many contrivances to protect her against enemy vessels; she carries a large supply of arms for the men, and contains a set of household utensils for each mess. In addition to all this, she is laden with cargo which the skipper carries for profit. And all the things I mention were contained in a chamber of little more than a hundred square cubits [The word δεκάκλινος is literally "having space for ten couches."] and I noticed that each kind of thing was so neatly stowed away that there was no confusion, no work for a searcher, nothing out of place, no troublesome untying to cause delay when anything was wanted for immediate use. I found that the steersman's servant, who is called the mate, knows each particular section so exactly, that he can tell even when away where everything is kept and how much there is of it, just as well as a man who knows how to spell can tell how many letters there are in Socrates and in what order they come. Now I saw this man in his spare time inspecting all the stores that are wanted, as a matter of course, in the ship ("during the voyage"). I was surprised to see him looking over them, and asked what he was doing. "Sir," he answered, "I am looking to see how the ship's tackle is stored, in case of accident, or whether anything is missing or mixed up with other stuff. For when God sends a storm at sea, there's no time to search about for what you want or to serve it out if it's in a muddle. For God threatens and punishes careless fellows, and you're lucky if he merely refrains from destroying the innocent; and if he saves you when you do your work well, you have much cause to thank heaven."

Now after seeing the ship's tackle in such perfect order, I told my wife: "Considering that folk aboard a merchant vessel, even though it be a little one, find room for things and keep order, though tossed violently to and fro, and find what they want to get, though terror-stricken, it would be downright carelessness on our part if we, who have large store rooms in our house to keep everything separate and whose house rests on solid ground, fail to find a good and handy place for everything. . . .

bibliography

Alexander, Gerard L. "Viking America: A New Theory." *American Heritage,* vol. XXIII, no. 5 (August 1972): 26-29, 106-9.

Al-Idrisi, Al Sharif. *India and the Neighbouring Territories.* Ed., intro. S. Magbul Ahmad. Leiden: E.J. Brill, 1960.

Al 'Omari, Ibn Fadl Allah. *Masalik el Absar fi Mamalik el Amsar. I. L'Afrique moins L'Egypte.* Tr. Gaudefroy-Demombynes. Paris: Librairie Orientaliste Paul Guenther, 1927.

Anderson, Rasmus B. *America not Discovered by Columbus.* Chicago, 1874.

_____. *The Flatey Book.* London: The Norroena Society, 1906. Icelandic text facsimiles with Icelandic transcription, Danish translation, English translation.

Anderson, Romola, and R.C. Anderson. *The Sailing Ship.* New York: Robert M. McBride's Company, 1947.

Andrews, Roy Chapman. *This Business of Exploring.* New York: G.P. Putnam's Sons, 1935.

Anon. "Greeks First to Discover America." *The Torch* (Dallas), vol. 3, no. 14 (August 1967): 1-2.

Anon. "The Queen Who Would be Different." *San Antonio Home and Club,* vol. IV, no. VII (January 1934).

Anon. "Village illuminates ancient life." San Antonio *Express,* April 23, 1976: 7D.

Anon. "The Visit of the Vikings." *Harper's New Monthly Magazine* LXV (June to November 1882): 515-27.

Anon. "Was Hanno discoverer of America?" Dallas *Times Herald,* April 16, 1975.

Arciniegas, Germán. *Amerigo and the New World.* New York: Alfred A. Knopf, 1955.

_____. "The Rediscovery of Amerigo." *Life,* October 11, 1954: 101f.

Ashe, Geoffrey, et al. *The Quest for America.* New York: Praeger Publishers, 1971.

Averdunk, H., and Dr. J. Müller-Reinhard. *Gerhard Mercator und die Geographen unter seinen Nachkommen.* Gotha: Justus Perthes, 1914.

Ayer, Alfred Jules. *Language, Truth & Logic.* New York: Dover Publishers, Inc., 1946.

Babcock, William H. *Legendary Islands of the Atlantic.* New York: American Geographical Society, 1922.

Bainbridge, William Sims. "Chariots of the Gullible." *The Skeptical Inquirer,* Winter 1978: 33-48.

Bancroft, Hubert Howe. *The Works of Hubert Howe Bancroft.* San Francisco: The History Co., Pub., 1886. See in particular: *The Native Races,* vol. I, and *The Native Races,* vol. V.

Bandelier, Adolph F., and Edgar L. Hewett. *Indians of the Rio Grande Valley.* New York: Cooper Square Publishers, Inc., 1973.

Barnard, Noel, ed. *Early Chinese Art and Its Possible Influence in the Pacific Basin.* 3 vols. New York: Intercultural Arts Press, 1972.

_____, and Sato Tamotsu. *Metallurgical Remains of Ancient China.* Tokyo: Nichiosha, 1975.

Barzun, Jacques, and Henry F. Graff. *The Modern Researcher.* New York: Harcourt, Brace Jovanovich, Inc., 1970.

Batalha-Reis, J. "The Supposed Discovery of South America Before 1448, and the Critical Methods of the Historians of Geographical Discovery." *Acta Cartographia* V: 1-26; from *Geographical Journal* XIX (1897): 185-210.

Baylor University. A Treasury of Maps from the holdings of the Texas Collection of Baylor University, an exhibit opening April 23, 1975. Waco, 1975.

Beazley, C. Raymond. *The Dawn of Modern Geography.* London: Henry Froude, Amen Corner, n.d.

Benavides, Antonio. "The Negro Colony Near Brownsville." Cameron County Scrapbook, Texas State Archives.

Benitez, Fernando. *In the Footsteps of Cortes.* London: Peter Owen, Ltd., 1957.

Bermant, Chaim, and Michael Weitzman. *Ebla, A Revelation in Archaeology.* New York: Times Books, 1979.

Blake, Edith. "The Astrolabe." *Sail,* vol. 3., no. 7 (July 1972): 64-65.

Blundeville, Thomas. *A Briefe Description of Universal Mappes and Cardes.* London, 1589; facsimile reprint, Amsterdam: Theatrum Orbis Terrarum Ltd, 1972.

Boas, Franz. *Language and Culture.* New York: MacMillan, 1940.

Boland, Charles Michael. *They All Discovered America.* Garden City, N.Y.: Doubleday & Company, Inc., 1961.

Bolton, Charles Knowles. *Terra Nova: The Northeast Coast of America Before 1602.* Boston: F.W. Faxon Co., 1935.

Bolton, Herbert Eugene. *Coronado, Knight of Pueblos and Plains.* Albuquerque: University of New Mexico Press, 1949; reprinted 1964.

———, ed. *Spanish Exploration in the Southwest.* New York: Barnes and Noble, Inc., 1908.

Bovill, E.W. *The Golden Trade of the Moors.* London: Oxford University Press, 1968.

Breuer, Hans. *Columbus Was Chinese.* New York: Herder and Herder, 1972. The English edition of *Kolumbus war Chinese,* 1970.

Brewington, M.V. *The Peabody Museum Collection of Navigational Instruments.* Salem, Mass.: Peabody Museum, 1963.

Brown, J. Macmillan. *The Riddle of the Pacific.* London: T. Fisher Unwin, Ltd., 1924.

Bruun, Daniel. *The Icelandic Colonization of Greenland and the Finding of Vinland.* København: Bianco Lunos Bogtrykkeri, 1918.

Bryan, J.P. *Ptolemy to Pressler: Milestones in Texas Cartography.* Exhibit catalogue, The Barker Texas History Center, The University of Texas at Austin, November 3, 1973.

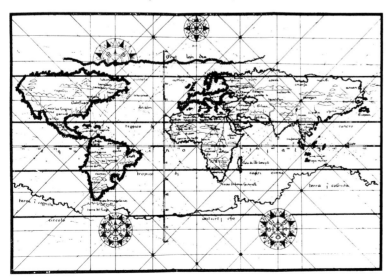

Bryan, James P., and Walter K. Hanak. *Texas in Maps.* Austin: The University of Texas, 1961.

Bryant, Vaughn M., Jr., and Harry J. Shafer. "The Late Quaternary Paleoenvironment of Texas: A Model for the Archeologist." *Bulletin of the Texas Archeological Society* 48 (1977): 1-25.

Burder, George, ed. *The Welch Indians or A Collection of Papers Respecting a People Whose Ancestors Emigrated from Wales to America, in the Year 1170, with Prince Madoc (Three Hundred Years Before the First Voyage of Columbus), And who are said now to inhabit a beautiful Country on the West Side of the Mississippi.* The Magazine of History, Extra Number—no. 78, Tarrytown, N.Y., reprinted 1922; originally issued, London: T. Chapman, 1787.

Caraci, Giuseppe. "The Reputed Inclusion of Florida in the Oldest Nautical Maps of the New World." *Imago Mundi* XV (1960): 32-39.

Caradoc (Caradog) of Llancarfan. See Powel, *The historie of Cambria.*

Carr, Edward Hallett. *What Is History?* New York: Vintage Books, 1961.

Cassidy, Vincent H. "Other Fortunate Islands and Some That Were Lost." *Terrae Incognitae* I: 35-39. Amsterdam: N. Israel, 1969.

Castañeda, Carlos E. *Our Catholic Heritage in Texas, 1519-1936.* Austin: Von Boeckmann-Jones Co., 1936.

Cazeau, Charles, and Stuart D. Scott Jr. *Exploring the Unknown.* New York and London: Plenum Press, 1979.

Chang, Kwang-Chih. *The Archaeology of Ancient China.* New Haven and London: Yale University Press, 1977.

—————. *Shang Civilization.* New Haven and London, Yale University Press, 1980.

Chapman, Charles E. *A History of California: The Spanish Period.* New York: The Macmillan Company, 1921.

Chapman, Paul H. *The Man Who Led Columbus to America.* Atlanta: Judson Press, 1973.

Chaucer, Geoffrey. *A Treatise on the Astrolabe.* Ed. Walter W. Skeat. London: Trubner & Co. for Chaucer Society, 1872 (manuscript of 1391).

Chinese Cultural Art Treasures. 3rd ed. Taipei, Republic of China: The National Palace Museum, 1967.

Chu, Daniel, and Elliott Skinner. *A Glorious Age in Africa.* New York: Doubleday & Co., Inc., 1965.

Cline, Donald. "The Los Lunas Stone." *Occasional Publications of the Epigraphic Society,* vol. 10, no. 238 (October 1982).

Cohen, Daniel. *Myths of the Space Age.* New York: Dodd, Mead & Company, 1967.

Cole, John R. Review of Jeffrey Goodman, "Psychic Archaeology." *The Skeptical Inquirer,* Spring/Summer 1978: 105-8.

————. "Anthropology Beyond the Fringe, Ancient Inscriptions, Early Man, and Scientific Method." *The Skeptical Inquirer,* Spring/Summer 1978: 62-71.

————. "Cult Archaeology and Unscientific Method and Theory." *Advances in Archaeological Method and Theory* 3: 1-33. Ed. Michael B. Schiffer. New York: Academic Press, 1980.

Collier, Christopher. "Who Discovered America?: A review of Recent Historiography." *The South Atlantic Quarterly* 66 (1967): 31-41.

Collinder, Per. *A History of Marine Navigation.* London, 1954.

Columbus. *The Journal of Christopher Columbus.* Tr. Cecil Jane. New York: Clarkson N. Potter, Inc.

Cortesad, Armando. *Portugaliae Monumenta Cartographica.* Lisbon, 1960.

Cotter, Charles H. *A History of Nautical Astronomy.* New York: American Elsevier Publishing Company, Inc., 1967.

Cousins, Norman. *Why Man Explores.* (A symposium held at the California Institute of Technology, Pasadena, July 2, 1976. Sponsored by National Aeronautics and Space Administration.) Washington, D.C.: Government Printing Office, n.d.

Covey, Cyclone. *Calalus: A Roman Jewish Colony in America From the Time of Charlemagne Through Alfred the Great.* New York: Vantage Press, 1975.

Coxe, William. *Account of the Russian Discoveries Between Asia and America. To which are added, The Conquest of Siberia, and The History of the Transactions and Commerce Between Russia and China.* London, 1780.

Creel, Herrlee Glessner. *The Birth of China.* New York: Frederick Ungar Publishing Co., 1937; 7th printing, 1970.

Crone, G.R. *The Discovery of America.* New York: Weybright and Talley, 1969.

Cuningham, William. *The Cosmographical Glasse.* London, 1559; facsimile reprint, Amsterdam and New York: Theatrum Orbis Terrarum Ltd. and Da Capo Press, 1968.

Davidson, Basil. *The Lost Cities of Africa.* Boston and Toronto: Little, Brown and Company, 1959.

Davies, Nigel. *Voyagers to the New World.* New York: William Morrow and Company, Inc., 1979.

Deacon, Richard. *Madoc and the Discovery of America.* New York: George Braziller, 1966.

Diodorus of Sicily. Tr. C.H. Oldfather. Loeb Classical Library. London: William Heinemann, Ltd.; New York: G.P. Putnam's Sons, 1933.

Dixon, Ford. "Maps and the Discovery of Texas—A Reexamination." *East Texas Historical Journal,* vol. V, no. 2 (October 1967): 101-3.

_____. "Texas History in Maps: An Archival and Historical Examination of the James Perry Bryan Map Collection." MA Thesis, Southwest Texas State College, August 1966.

Donnelly, Ignatius. *Atlantis: The Antediluvian World.* 1882; reprint, London: Sidgwick & Jackson, Ltd., 1950.

Dougherty, Dr. C.N. *Valley of the Giants.* Cleburne: Bennett Printing Co., 1971.

Eden, Richard. *The first Three English books on America.* Ed. Edward Arber. New York: Scribner & Welford, n.d.

Epstein, Jeremiah F. "Pre-Columbian Old World Coins in America: An Examination of the Evidence." *Current Anthropology,* vol. 21, no. 1 (February 1980): 1-20.

Fang Zhongpu. "Did Chinese Buddhists Reach America 1,000 Years Before Columbus?" *China Reconstructs,* vol. 29, no. 8 (August 1980): 65-66.

Farley, Gloria. "The Vikings Were Here." *Heavener, Oklahoma Adventureland.* [n.p.] August 1974.

Farmer, John. "Pineda's Sketch." *SHQ* 63 (July 1959-April 1960): 110-14.

Fell, Barry. *America B.C.* New York: Pocket Books, 1976.

_____. *Saga America.* New York: Times Books, 1980.

_____. "Stephens County, Texas—An Ogam Cave Inscription." *Occasional Publications of the Epigraphic Society,* vol. 10, part I, no. 247 (October 1982).

Fischer, Joseph. *The Discoveries of the Norsemen in America.* Tr. Basil H. Soulsby. London: Henny Stephens, Son & Stiles, 1903.

Fiske, John. *The Discovery of America.* 2 vols. Boston and New York: Houghton, Mifflin and Company, 1892.

Fitzgerald, Maurice, ed. *Poems of Robert Southey.* London: Henry Froude, Oxford University Press, 1909.

Flatey Book, The. London: Norroena Society, 1906.

Fleming, Thomas. "Evidence Proves It: Columbus Was a Latecomer." *Family Weekly,* January 29, 1978: 16.

Flint, Richard Foster. *Glacial Geology and the Pleistocene Epoch.* New York: John Wiley & Sons, Inc., 1947.

Flores, Anselmo Marino. "Indian Population and Its Identification." *Handbook of Middle American Indians,* vol. 6. Ed. Robert Wauchope. Social anthropology. Austin: University of Texas Press, 1967.

Frakes, L.A. *Climates Throughout Geologic Time.* Amsterdam, Oxford, New York: Elsevier Scientific Publishing Co., 1979.

Fraser, John. *History and Etymology.* Oxford: Clarendon Press, 1932.

Frost, Frank J. "The Palos Verdes Chinese Anchor Mystery." *Archeology,* January/February 1982: 22-28.

Gallois, L. "Le Portulan de Nicolas de Canerio." *Acta Cartographia* IX: 76-98; from *Bulletin de la Societe de Geographie de Lyon* IX, 1890: 97-119.

Galvano, Antonie (Antonio Galvão). *The Discoveries of the World.* London, 1601; facsimile reprint, Amsterdam and New York: Theatrum Orbis Terrarum Ltd. and Da Capo Press, 1969.

Giles, H.A. *The Travels of Fa-Hsien.* London: Routledge & Kegan Paul, 1923.

Gladwin, Harold Sterling. *Men Out of Asia.* New York: McGraw-Hill Book Company, Inc., 1947.

Gomara, L. *La historia general de las Indias.* Anvers, 1554.

Goodman, Jeffrey. *American Genesis.* New York: Summit Books, 1981.

_____. *Psychic Archaeology.* New York: G.P. Putnam's Sons, 1977.

Gordon, Cyrus H. *Before Columbus.* New York: Crown Publishers, Inc., 1971.

Gottschalk, Louis. *Understanding History.* New York: Knopf, 1969.

Gould, Rupert T. *The Marine Chronometer.* London: The Holland Press.

Greene, David. *The Irish Language.* Dublin: Cultural Relations Committee of Ireland at the Three Candles, Ltd., 1966.

Hakluyt, Richard. *The Principall Navigations, Voiages and Discoveries of the English nation, made by Sea or over Land, to the most remote and farthest distant Quarters of the earth at any time within the compasse of these 1500 yeeres* . . . London: George Bishop and Ralph Newberie, 1589. A convenient edition is the Glasgow of 1904.

Ham, William E. "Geological Report on the Heavener 'Rune Stone.' " *The Chronicles of Oklahoma,* vol. 37, no. 4 (Winter 1959-1960): 506-7.

Hapgood, Charles H. *Maps of the Ancient Sea Kings.* Philadelphia and New York: Chilton Books, 1966.

Harden, Donald. *The Phoenicians.* London: Thames and Hudson, 1962.

Harding, Louis Allen. *A Brief History of the Art of Navigation.* New York: The William-Frederick Press, 1952.

Haring, Clarence Henry. *Trade and Navigation Between Spain and the Indies in the Time of the Hapsburgs.* 2nd ed. Gloucester, Mass.: Peter Smith, 1964.

Harris, Neill J. "The Riddle of America's Elephant Slabs." *Science Digest,* vol. 69, no. 3 (March 1971): 74-77.

Harrisse, Henry. *The Discovery of North America.* Amsterdam: N. Israel, 1961.

Hartwig, Georg L. *The Polar and Tropical Worlds.*

Hawthorne, Julian. *Spanish America.* New York: Peter Fenelon Collier, 1899.

Heawood, Edward. "The World Map Before and After Magellan's Voyage." *Acta Cartographia* XI: 203-26; from *Geographical Journal* LVII, 1921: 431-46.

Heeren, A[rnold] H[ermann] L[udwig]. *Historical Researches Into the Politics, Intercourse, and Trade of the Carthaginians, Ethiopians, and Egyptians.* 1832; reprint, New York: Negro Universities Press, 1969.

Heine-Geldern, Robert. "The Problem of Transpacific Influences in Mesoamerica." *Handbook of Middle American Indians* 4: 277-95. Austin: University of Texas Press, 1966.

————. "Ein römischer Fund aus dem vorkolumbischen Mexiko." *Anzeiger der Österreichischen Akademie der Wissenschaften* (Philosophisch-Historische Klasse), no. 16 (1961): 117-19.

Hennig, Richard. "Arabische 'Abenteurer' im Atlantischen Ozean." *Terrae Incognitae:* 113. Leiden: E.J. Brill, 1950.

————. "Der Buddhistenmönch Hui-Schen in 'Fusang.'" *Terrae Incognitae:* 33-41. Leiden: E.J. Brill, 1950.

————. "Eines Neger-Sultans Erkundungsfahrten im Atlantischen Ozean." *Terrae Incognitae:* 132. Leiden: E.J. Brill, 1950.

Herm, Gerhard. *The Phoenicians, the Purple Empire of the Ancient World.* New York: William Morrow and Company, Inc., 1975.

Herodotus. Tr. A.D. Godley. Loeb Classical Library. Cambridge, Mass.: Harvard University Press; London: William Heinemann Ltd., 1916.

Herrmann, Paul. *Conquest by Man.* Tr. Michael Bullock. New York: Harper & Brothers, 1954.

Hill, Lawrence Francis. *José de Escandón and the Founding of Nuevo Santander.* Columbus: Ohio State University Press, 1926.

Hirth, F[riedrich]. *China and the Roman Orient.* 1885; reprint, Shanghai and Hong Kong: Kelly & Walsh, 1939.

————, and W.W. Rockhill, trs. and eds. *Chau Ju-kua: His Work on the Chinese and Arab Trade in the Twelfth and Thirteenth Centuries, entitled Chu-fan-chï.* Amsterdam: Oriental Press, 1966.

Ho, Ping-Ti. *The Cradle of the East.* Hong Kong: Chinese University of Hong Kong, University of Chicago Press, 1975.

Hodge, Frederick W., ed. *Spanish Explorers in the Southern United States 1528-1543.* New York: Barnes & Noble, Inc., 1907; reprint, 1965.

Hoffman, Bernard G. *Cabot to Cartier, Sources for a Historical Ethnography of Northeastern North America, 1497-1550.* Toronto: University of Toronto Press.

Holand, Hjalmar R. *Explorations in America before Columbus.* New York, 1956.

————. *The Kensington Stone.* Ephraim, 1932.

————. *A Pre-Columbian Crusade to America.* New York, 1962.

_____. *Westward from Vineland.* New York, 1940.

Holman, Louis A. *Old Maps and Their Makers.* Boston: Charles E. Goodspeed & Co., 1925.

Holmes. W.H. *Handbook of Aboriginal American Antiquities, Part I, Introductory, The Lithic Industries.* Washington, D.C.: Smithsonian Institution, Bureau of American Ethnology, 1919.

_____. *Art in Shell.* 2nd Annual Report of Bureau of Ethnology to Secretary of the Smithsonian, 1880-81: 286f. Washington, D.C., 1883.

Hooton, Earnest Albert. *Apes, Men, and Morons.* 1937; reprint, Freeport, N.Y.: Books for Libraries Press, 1970.

Hopkins, L.C. "The Sovereigns of the Shang Dynasty." *Journal of the Royal Asiatic Society,* 1917: 70-89.

Horgan, Paul. *Conquistadores in North America.* London: Macmillan & Co. Ltd., 1963.

Hornell, James. "British Coracles." *The Mariner's Mirror,* vol. XXII, no. 1 (January 1936): 5-41; vol. XXII, no. 3 (July 1936): 261-304.

Howell, George Rogers. "The Globe of 1513, and the Progress of Geographical Discovery and Mapmaking From the Time of Columbus to 1600." *Acta Cartographia* VI: 199-222; from *Transactions of the Albany Institute* XII (1893): 241-50.

Hwui Shan. The Account of Hwui Shan is recorded in the Liang-shu (The Records of the Liang Dynasty) as part of the Nan-shi (or Nan-szu, the History of the South) compiled by Li Yen-shau (Li Yan Chu) in the seventh century A.D.

   The Nan-shi is part of the Great Annals of China, or "Twenty-two Historians," the Nien-rh-shi.

   It was copied (and apparently somewhat amended) by Ma Twan-lin in his Wan-hien T'ung-k'au (or Wan Hsien Tung Kao, "A Thorough Examination into Antiquity" or "Antiquarian Researches"), c. 1321 +.

   Ma Twan-lin's work, composed of three hundred forty-eight chapters, recounts Hwui Shan's story under the last title, Sz' I Kao, or "Researches into the Four Frontiers," as part of the last twenty-four chapters. His version is quoted in Edward P. Vining's *An Inglorious Columbus.*

   Hwui Shan's interrogator, Yu-kie, left his own version in the Liang-sse-kong-ki, the "Report of the Four Lords of the Liang Dynasty."

Hyde, Walter Woodburn. *Ancient Greek Mariners.* New York: Oxford University Press, 1947.

Imbert, Enrique Anderson. "Raconteurs of the Conquest." *Américas,* August 1972.

Ingstad, Helge. *Westward to Vinland.* New York: St. Martin's Press, 1969.

Jairazbhoy, R.A. *Ancient Egyptians and Chinese in America.* Totowa, N.J.: Roman and Littlefield, 1974.

Jane, Cecil, tr. *The Journal of Christopher Columbus.* New York: Clarkson N. Potter, Inc.

Jeffreys, D.W. "Pre-Columbian Negroes in America." *Scientia,* vol. LXXXVIII, n. CDXCV-VI, VII-VIII-1953: 202-18.

Jeffreys, M.D.W. "Pre-Columbian Arabs in the Caribbean." *The Mushins Digest,* August 1954: 25-29.

Jennings, Jesse D. *Prehistory of North America.* New York: McGraw-Hill Book Company, 1968.

Johnson, Elmer H. *The Natural Regions of Texas.* The University of Texas Bulletin no. 3113 (April 1, 1931; reprint, 1952).

Johnston, Thomas Crawford. *Did the Phoenicians Discover America?* London: James Niset & Co., Ltd., 1913.

Jones, Gwyn. *The Norse Atlantic Saga.* London, 1964.

————. *A History of the Vikings.* London: Oxford University Press, 1968.

Kan, C.M. "De Periplous van Hanno." *Acta Cartographia* XII (1971): 184-237; from *Tijdschrift van het Kon. Nederlandsch Aardrijkskundig Genootschap,* 2e serie, VIII, 1891: 598-651.

Keightley, David N. *Sources of Shang History, The Oracle-Bone Inscriptions of Bronze Age China.* Berkeley: University of California Press, 1978.

Kelly, John. *A Practical Grammar of the Ancient Gaelic or Language of the Isle of Man, Usually Called Manks.* Douglas, Isle of Man, 1859.

Kennedy, J. "The Gospels of the Infancy. . . ." *Journal of the Royal Asiatic Society,* 1917: 209-43, 469-540.

King, Barbara C. "Who discovered America." *Grade Teacher,* October 1971: 38-40.

Kirkland, Forrest, and W.W. Newcomb Jr. *The Rock Art of Texas Indians.* Austin and London: University of Texas Press, 1967.

Kish, George, ed. *A Source Book in Geography.* Cambridge: Harvard University Press, 1978.

Kohl, J.G. "Charts of the Northmen." *Acta Cartographia* V: 337f; from *Collection of the Maine Historical Society,* 1869: 107-10.

Krause, Wolfgang. *Runeninschriften im Älteren Futhark.* Halle: Max Niemeyer, 1937.

Lafitau, J.F. *Moeurs des sauvages comparees aux moeurs des premiers temps.* Paris, 1723.

Lamb, Ursula. "Science by Litigation: A Cosmographic Feud." *Terrae Incognitae* I: 40-57. Amsterdam: N. Israel, 1969.

Landsverk, O.G. "Norsemen in Oklahoma." *Oklahoma Today,* vol. 20, no. 3 (Summer 1970): 28-36.

Larson, Robert. "Was America the Wonderful Land of Fusang?" *American Heritage* 17, 3 (1966).

Legge, James, tr. "The Travels of Fâ-Hien." *Chinese Literature:* 203-77. Ed. Epiphanius Wilson. New York: The Colonial Press, 1902.

Leland, Charles G. *Fusang.* 1875; reprint, London: Curzon Press, 1973.

Levillier, Roberto. "New Light on Vespucci's Third Voyage." *Imago Mundi* XI (1955): 37-46.

Li, Chi. *The Beginnings of Chinese Civilization.* Seattle: University of Washington Press, 1957.

Li, Dun J. *The Ageless Chinese.* New York: Charles Scribner's Sons, 1965 (1971).

Li, Hui-Lin. "Mu-Lan-P'i: A Case For Pre-Columbian Trans-atlantic Travel by Arab Ships." *Harvard Journal of Asiatic Studies* 23 (1961): 114-26.

Loehr, Max. *Chinese Bronze Age Weapons.* Ann Arbor: University of Michigan Press, 1956.

_____. *Relics of Ancient China.* New York: Asia Society, 1965.

_____. *Ritual Vessels of Bronze Age China.* New York: Asia Society, 1968.

Loewe, Michael. "Spices and Silk: Aspects of World Trade in the First Seven Centuries of the Christian Era." *Journal of the Royal Asiatic Society,* no. 2 (1971): 166-79.

_____. "The Wooden and Bamboo Strips Found at Mo-Chu-Tzu (Kansu)." *Journal of the Royal Asiatic Society,* parts 1 and 2 (1965): 13-26.

Lommel, Andreas. *Prehistoric and Primitive Man.* New York: McGraw-Hill Book Co., 1966.

Long, John. "State Runes Child's Play." *The Oklahoma Journal,* vol. 19, no. 7 (October 7, 1971).

Lossing, B.J. *Pictorial Field Book of the Revolution.* 2 vols. New York: Harpers, 1859.

Lowe, C.H. "Books and Printing in China, Before Gutenberg." *Chinese Culture,* vol. XX, no. 2 (June 1979): 111-23.

Lowery, Woodbury. *The Lowery Collection. A Descriptive List of Maps of the Spanish Possessions within the Present Limits of the United States, 1502-1820.* Washington, D.C.: Government Printing Office, 1912.

_____. *The Spanish Settlements Within the Present Limits of the United States.* New York: Russell & Russell, Inc., 1959.

Lowie, Robert. *The History of Ethnological Theory.* New York: Holt, Reinhart, and Winston, 1966.

Lummis, Charles F. *The Spanish Pioneers.* Chicago: A.C. McClurg & Co., 1918.

Luo Rongqu. "Legends, Stone Anchors, and the 'Chinese Columbus' Theory." *China Reconstructs,* vol. XXXII, no. 4 (April 1983): 8-9.

McDermott, John Francis. "America." *Missouri Historical Society Bulletin* XI (1955): 371-78.

McGee, Bernice, and Jack McGee. "Mystery Tablet of the Big Bend." *True West,* vol. 19, no. 6 (whole no. 112) (July-August 1972): 10-15, 42-48.

————. "Runestones and Tombstones." *Old West,* Winter 1969: 13-18, 60-67.

McGregor, John C. *Southwestern Archaeology.* Urbana: University of Illinois Press, 1965.

Mackenzie, Donald A. *Myths of Pre-Columbian America.* London: Gresham Publishing Co. Ltd., 1924.

McKern, Sharon S. *Exploring the Unknown.* New York: Praeger Publishers, 1972.

Magnus, Olaus. *Historia de Gentibus Septentrionalibus.* 1555; facsimile reprint, Copenhagen: Rosenkilde and Bagger, 1972.

Mallery, Arlington, and Mary Roberts Harrison. *The Rediscovery of Lost America.* New York: E.P. Dutton, 1979.

Marble, Samuel D. *Before Columbus.* South Brunswick and New York: A.S. Barnes and Company, 1980.

Marcus, G[eoffrey] J[ules]. *The Conquest of the North Atlantic.* New York: Oxford University Press, 1981.

Marschall, Wolfgang. *Transpazifische Kulturbeziehungen.* München: Klaus Renner Verlag, 1972.

Martyr, Peter. English translation, see Eden, Richard.

Marx, Eric. "Egyptian Shipping." *Mariner's Mirror* 33 (1947): 139-69.

Maxwell, Ross A. *The Big Bend of the Rio Grande.* 3rd ed. Austin: The University of Texas at Austin, Bureau of Economic Geology, 1971.

Meggers, Betty J. *Prehistoric America.* Chicago: Aldine Publishing Company, 1972.

————, Clifford Evans and Emilio Estrada. *Early Formative Period of Coastal Ecuador: The Valdivia and Machalilla Phases.* Washington, D.C.: Smithsonian Institution, 1965.

Mertz, Henriette. *Atlantis, Dwelling Place of the Gods.* (Privately printed) Chicago, Ill. 60690: Box 207, Loop Station, 1976.

————. *Pale Ink, Two Ancient Records of Chinese Exploration in America.* Chicago: Swallow Press, 1972.

Mills, J.V. "Notes on Early Chinese Voyages." *Journal of the Royal Asiatic Society,* parts 1 and 2 (1951): 3-25.

Morgan, Lewis. *Ancient Society.* New York: Henry Holt, 1878.

Morison, Samuel Eliot. *Portuguese Voyages to America in the Fifteenth Century.* New York: Octagon Books, Inc., 1965.

Moscati, Sabatino. *The World of the Phoenicians.* New York: Frederick A. Praeger, 1968.

Mostra Vespucciana (Catalog). An exhibition (index, catalogs of materials) on the fifth centenary of the birth of Vespucci. Firenze, 1755.

Mowat, Farley. *Westviking.* Boston: Little, Brown and Company.

Myres, John L. "An Attempt to Reconstruct the Maps Used by Herodotus." *Acta Cartographia* III: 418-44; from *Geographical Journal* VIII (1896): 605-31.

Needham, Joseph. *Science and Civilization in China.* Cambridge: At the University Press, 1954.

Noorbergen, Rene. "Did the Chinese Discover America 4,000 Years Before Columbus." *The* (London) *Sunday Express,* June 14, 1979: 8.

Nordenskiöld, A.E. "Résumé of an Essay on the Early History of Charts and Sailing Directions." *Acta Cartographia* XVII (1973): 185-94; from the Report of the Sixth International Geographical Congress, London, 1895-1896: 685-94.

North, J.D. "The Astrolabe." *Scientific American,* January 1974: 96-106.

Obregon, Mauricio. *Argonauts to Astronauts.* New York: Harper & Row, 1980.

Oldham, H. Yule. "The Importance of Mediaeval Manuscript Maps in the Study of the History of Geographical Discovery." *Acta Cartographia* XVII (1973): 101-4; from the Report of the Sixth International Geographical Congress, London, 1895-1896: 703-6.

————. "A Pre-Columbian Discovery of America," paper presented at the Royal Geographical Society, Technical Meeting, November 1894. *Geographical Journal,* no. III (March 1895).

Palacio, Diego Garcia de. *Instruccion Nautica para Navegar.* 1587; facsimile reprint, Madrid: Ediciones Cultura Hispanica, 1944.

Parry, J.H. *The Age of Reconnaissance.* New York: Mentor Books, New American Library, 1963.

————. *The Discovery of the Sea.* New York: The Dial Press, 1974.

Perkins, Dixie L. *The Meaning of the New Mexico Mystery Stone.* Albuquerque: Sun Publishing Co., 1979.

Pistilli S., Ingeniero don Vicente. *Vikingos en el Paraguay.* Asuncion, 1978.

[Plutarch] Goodwin, William W. *Plutarch's Morals,* vol. V. London: The Athenaeum Press, 1870. "Of the face appearing within the orb of the moon," tr. "A.G. Gent."

Pohl, Frederick J. *Amerigo Vespucci, Pilot Major.* New York: Columbia University Press, 1944.

_____. *The Lost Discovery.* New York: W.W. Norton & Co., 1952.

Powel, David. *The historie of Cambria, now called Wales.* London, 1584; facsimile reprint, Amsterdam and New York: Theatrum Orbis Terrarum Ltd. and Da Capo Press, 1969.

Quatrefages, A. de. *The Human Species.* New York: D. Appleton and Company, 1883.

Quinn, David B. "The Argument for the English Discovery of America Between 1480 and 1494." *Geographical Journal* 127 (1961): 277-85.

Richardson, T.C. "When the Norsemen Came to Texas. . . ." *Farm and Ranch,* vol. 45, no. 34 (August 21, 1926): 1, 10-11.

Riley, Carroll L., et al., eds. *Man across the Sea.* Austin and London: University of Texas Press, 1971.

Robinson, Tess. "3,000 Years Before Columbus." *Buffalo,* vol. II, no. 2 (March 1981): 16-20.

Rosínska, Grażyna. *Instrumenty Astronomiczne na Uniwersytecie Krakowskim W XV Wieku.* Wrocław, 1974.

Roukema, E. "A Discovery of Yucatan prior to 1503." *Imago Mundi* XIII: 30-38.

_____. "The Mythical 'First Voyage' of the *Soderini Letter.*" *Imago Mundi* XVI (1962): 70-75.

Sahagún, Bernardino de. *General History of the things of New Spain.* Santa Fe: School of American Research, 1950; 2nd rev. ed. 1975.

_____. *Historia general de las casas de Nueva España.* México: Impr. del ciudadano A. Valdés, 1829-1830.

Sauer, Carl Ortwin. *Sixteenth Century North America.* Berkeley: University of California Press, 1971.

Saunders, Harold N. *The Astrolabe.* Teignmouth, Devon.: Brunswick Press, Ltd., 1971.

Schmidt, F. "On the Discovery of North America by the Scandinavians, about the year 986." *The Analectic Magazine,* n.s., vol. II, no. IV (October 1820): 267-88. Tr. from *Svea* by F.H. Schroeder.

Schmidt, Wilhelm. *The Culture Historical Method of Ethnology.* Tr. S.A. Sieber. New York: Fortuny's, 1939.

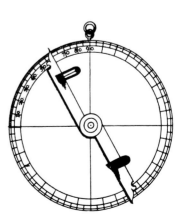

Schoenwetter, James, and Frank W. Eddy. *Alluvial and Palynological Reconstruction of Environments.* Santa Fe: Museum of New Mexico, 1964.

Schwartz, Seymour I, and Ralph E. Ehrenberg. *The Mapping of America.* New York: Harry N. Abrams, 1980.

Schwerin, Karl H. *Winds Across the Atlantic.* Mesoamerican Studies Number 6. Carbondale: University Museum, Southern Illinois University, 1970.

Scofield, John. "Christopher Columbus and the New World He Found." *National Geographic,* vol. 148, no. 5 (November 1975): 584-625.

Selmer, Carl. *Navigatio Sancti Brendani Abbatis.* Publications in Mediaeval Studies XVI. Notre Dame: University of Notre Dame Press, 1959.

Severin, Tim. *The Brendan Voyage.* New York: McGraw-Hill Book Company, 1978.

Shan Hai King (The Classic of Mountains and Seas). The books are available to the present day as reprints. Sections concerned with the land traverses in the far east are: the Fourth Book, "Classic of the Eastern Mountains"; the Ninth Book, "Classic of the regions beyond the Eastern Sea"; and the Fourteenth Book, "Classic of the great Eastern waste."

Shao, Paul. *Asiatic Influences in Pre-Columbian American Art.* Ames: Iowa State University Press, 1976.

Silverberg, Robert. *Mound Builders of Ancient America: the Archaeology of a Myth.* Greenwich, Conn.: New York Graphic Society, 1968.

Skeeli, Lydia Lowndes Maury. *An Ethnohistorical Survey of Texas Indians.* Austin: Texas Historical Survey Committee, Report Number 22, October 1972.

Southey, Robert. *Madoc.* London: Longman, 1807.

Spence, Lewis. *The History of Atlantis.* 1926; reprint, University Books, 1968.

_____. *The Problem of Atlantis.* New York: Brentano's, 1924.

Steiner, Stan. *Fusang, The Chinese Who Built America.* New York: Harper & Row, 1979.

Stevenson, Edward Luther. *Early Spanish Cartography of the New World.* (Reprinted from the Proceedings of the American Antiquarian Society, April 1909.) Worchester, Mass.: Davis Press, 1909.

_____. *Marine World Chart of Nicolo de Canerio Januensis, 1502.* New York: The American Geographical Society and The Hispanic Society of America, 1908.

_____. *Portolan Charts.* New York: The Hispanic Society of America, 1911.

Stevenson, E.L. "Typical Early Maps of the New World." *Acta Cartographia* XII: 449-71; from the Bulletin of the American Geographical Society of New York XXXIX (1907): 202-24.

Stonebreaker, Jay, "A Decipherment of the Los Lunas Decalogue Inscription." *Occasional Publications of the Epigraphic Society,* vol. 10, no. 239 (October 1982).

Story, Ronald. *Guardians of the Universe.* New York: St. Martin's Press, 1980.

_____. *The Space-Gods Revealed.* New York: Harper & Row, 1976.

Strabo. *The Geography of Strabo.* Tr. Horace Leonard Jones. Loeb Classical Library. 1917; reprint, London: William Heinemann, Ltd., 1960.

Sølver, Carl V. "Egyptian Shipping of About 1500 B.C." *The Mariner's Mirror,* vol. XXII, no. 4 (October 1936): 430-69.

_____. *Vestervejen om Vikingernes Sejlads.* København: Iver C. Weilbach & Co., 1954.

Taylor, Edward. *Primitive Culture.* 1871; reprint, New York: Harper Torchbook, 1958.

_____. *Researches into the Early History of Mankind and the Development of Civilization.* New York: Henry Holt, 1878 (1865).

Taylor, E[va] G[ermaine] R[inington]. *The Haven-Finding Art.*

_____. *Mathematics and the Navigator in the Thirteenth Century.* London: The Institute of Navigation (lecture of October 22, 1959).

Taylor, Herbert C., Jr. "Vinland and the Way Thither." *Man Across the Sea.* Ed. Carroll L. Riley, et al. Austin: University of Texas Press, 1971: 242-54.

"Texas Collection." *SHQ* LVIII (July 1954-April 1955): 562-63. (A note reported from member Daniel Donoghue pointing out recognition of C. Arciniegas's *Life* article concerning Amerigo's possible visit to the Texas coast.)

Texas State Highway Department. *General Highway Maps,* 1974.

Thomson, Ron B., ed., intro., tr. *Jordanus de Nemore and the Mathematics of Astrolabes: De Plana Sphera.* Toronto: Pontifical Institute of Medieval Studies, 1978.

Tibbetts, G.R. *Arab Navigation in the Indian Ocean Before the Coming of the Portuguese.* London: The Royal Asiatic Society of Great Britain and Ireland, 1971.

Todd, Neil B. "Cats and Commerce." *Scientific American,* vol. 237, no. 5 (November 1977): 100-107.

Tolbert, Frank X. "Track of the Man-like Giant Under Waterfall." *Dallas Morning News,* January 6, 1973.

Tooley, R. Vand, and Charles Bricker. *Landmarks of Mapmaking.* New York: Thomas Y. Crowell Co., 1976 (1968).

Tornöe J[ohannes] Kr.[istoffer]. *Norsemen Before Columbus.* London: George Allen & Unwin, Ltd., 1965.

Totten, Norman. "Archeology and Epigraphy in America, Confrontation or Cooperation?" *Occasional Publications of the Epigraphic Society,* vol. 9, no. 209 (June 1981): 15-22.

Trento, Salvatore Michael. *The Search for Lost America.* Chicago: Contemporary Books, Inc., 1978.

True, David O. "Some Early Maps Relating to Florida." *Imago Mundi* XI: 72-84.

Underwood, L. Lyle. "The Los Lunas Inscription." *Occasional Publications of the Epigraphic Society,* vol. 10, no. 237 (October 1982).

United States Army, Corps of Engineers, Army Map Service. Western United States Series: NH 13-5 Marfa; NH 13-8 Presidio; NH 13-9 Emory Peak.

Valentini, Ph. "A New and an Ancient Map of Yucatan." *Acta Cartographia:* 463-67; from *The Magazine of American History* III, 1879: 295-99.

Van Sertima, Ivan. *They Came Before Columbus.* New York: Random House, 1976.

Verwey, D. "Could Ancient Ships Work to Windward?" *Queries,* in *The Mariner's Mirror,* vol. XXII, no. I (January 1936): 117.

Vespucci. "Amerigo Vespucci's Account of his Third Voyage." *Old South Leaflets,* vol. IV, no. 90: 1-16. Boston: Directors of the Old South Works, 1896.

Vining, Edward P. *An Inglorious Columbus.* New York: D. Appleton and Co., 1885.

Waldseemüller, Martin. *Cosmographiae Introductio.* Ann Arbor: University Microfilms, Inc.

Wallace, Birgitta L. "Some Points of Controversy." *The Quest for America.* Geoffrey Ashe, et al. New York: Praeger: 155-74.

Walsh, W.H. *Philosophy of History.* New York: Harper & Row, 1960.

Washburn, Wilcomb E. A review of Arciniegas's *Amerigo and the New World,* and a lively subsequent exchange of comment by Arciniegas in "Reviews of Books." *William and Mary Quarterly* XII (1956): 102-7, 448-53.

Waters, David W. *The Art of Navigation in England in Elizabethan and Early Stuart Times.* London: Hollis and Carter, 1958.

Waters, Frank. *Book of the Hopi.* New York: The Viking Press, 1963.

Watkins, Patsy. "Ancient Roman Coin Found near Round Rock." *Texas Times,* January 1977: 3.

Watson, William. *Archeology in China.* London: Parrish, 1960.

————. *China Before the Han Dynasty.* New York: Frederick A. Praeger, 1961.

————. *Early Civilization in China.* New York: McGraw-Hill, 1966.

Wauchope, Robert. *Lost Tribes & Sunken Continents.* Chicago: University of Chicago Press, 1962.

Wendorf, Fred, ed. *Paleoecology of the Llano Estacado.* Santa Fe: Museum of New Mexico Press, 1961.

Whipple, A.W., Thomas Eubank, and William W. Turner. *Report upon the Indian Tribes, in Reports of Explorations and Surveys to Ascertain the Most Practicable and Economical Route for a Railroad from the Mississippi River to the Pacific Ocean.* 33rd Congress, 2nd Session, Senate Ex. Doc. no. 78, 1856, vol. III; also House of Representatives Ex. Doc. no. 91, vol. III. Washington, D.C.: Government Printing Office, 1856.

Wieger, L. *Chinese Characters.* New York: Paragon Reprint Corp., 1965.

Wiener, Leo. *Africa and the Discovery of America.* 3 vols. 1922; reprint, New York: Kraus Reprint Co., 1971.

Williams, Brad, and Choral Pepper. *The Mysterious West.* Cleveland and New York: World Publishing Company, 1967.

Williams, S. Wells. *A Syllabic Dictionary of the Chinese Language.* Shanghai, 1874.

Winter, Heinrich. "The Origin of the Sea Chart." *Imago Mundi* XIII: 39-44.

Wright, Richard R. "Negro Companions of the Spanish Explorers." *Phylon,* vol. II, no. 4 (Fourth Quarter 1941): 325-36.

Wuthenau, Alexander von. *The Art of Terracotta Pottery in Pre-Columbian Central and South America.* New York: Crown Publishers, Inc., 1969. (English ed. of 1965 original German.)

————. *Unexpected Faces in Ancient America.* New York: Crown Publishers, Inc., 1975.

Wyckoff, Don. "The Vikings in Oklahoma; A Look At A Controversy." *Sulphur Times-Democrat,* October 7, 1971.

Xenophon. *Oeconomicus.* Tr. E.C. Marchant. Loeb Classical Library. London: William Heinemann; New York: G.P. Putnam's Sons, 1923.

Young, Ching-chi. "The Art of Chinese Writing." *Asia and the Americas,* January 1945: 23-28.

Zéndegui, Guillermo de. "The Rediscovery: Goals and Attainments." *Américas,* August 1972.

Zweig, Stefan. *Amerigo, A Comedy of Errors in History.* New York: Viking Press, 1942.

Early idea of iguanas in New World

iLLUSTRATiON CREDiTS

Page 40 Hieronymo Girava, *Dos Libros de Cosmographia* (Milan, 1556).

Page 43 Konrad Kretschmer, *Historia de la Geografía* (Barcelona: Editorial Labor, 1942).

Page 45 Dave Garrison, San Antonio.

Page 46 Pedro de Medina, *Regimiento de Navegacion,* 1543.

Page 49 Tom Guderjan, San Antonio.

Page 52 F. Whymper, *The Sea* (London: Cassell, Petter, Calpin and Co., n.d.).

Page 56 Mermaid: Pieter Aa, *Naaukeurige Versameling der Gedenk-Waardigste Zee en Land-Reyser na Oost en West-Indiën* (Leyden, 1707), volume XXV.

Page 58 Philoponus, *Nova typis . . .,* plate 4.

Page 59 Philoponus, *Nova typis. . . .*

Page 62 F. Whymper, *The Sea, . . .,* page 300.

Page 63 *Harper's New Monthly Magazine* (New York: Harper and Brothers, 1883), volume 66, page 224.

Page 65 Richard Hakluyt, *The Principall Navigations, Voiages and Discoveries of the English nation, made by Sea or over Land, to the most remote and farthest distant Quarters of the earth at any time within the compass of these 1500 yeeres . . .*(London: George Bishop and Ralph Newberie, 1589).

Page 66 Olaus Magnus, *Historia de Gentibus. . . .*

Page 68 *Harper's Weekly,* September 23, 1875, pages 780-81.

Page 71 Pieter Aa, *Naaukeurige Versameling . . .,* volume II, facing page 7.

Page 72 Pieter Aa, *Naaukeurige Versameling . . .,* volume I.

Page 74 *The Mirror,* Saturday, April 10, 1830, volume XV, number 423, page 241.

Page 75 Francisco Vindel, *Mapas de America. . . .*

Page 76 Gio. Ramusio, *Delle Navigationi et Viaggi,* Venetia, MDCVI.

Page 77 F. Whymper, *The Sea. . . .*

Page 79 Pieter Aa, *Naaukeurige Versameling . . .,* volume II, page 41.

Page 82 Pieter Aa, *Naaukeurige Versameling . . .,* volume X, facing page 1.

Page 83 Pedro de Medina, *Arte de Navigar* (Valladolid, 1545).

Page 85 Hieronymo Girava, *Dos Libros . . .,* title page.

Page 86 *Holländischer Kupferstich aus dem 16 Jarhundert.* Photo OSIS.

Page 87 Jules Verne, *The Exploration . . .,* page 207.

Page 88 Bruce Marshall, Institute of Texan Cultures Collection.

Page 89 Frederick J. Pohl, *Amerigo Vespucci, Pilot Major* (New York: Columbia University Press, 1944).

Page 90 Engraving in the Galleria degli Uffizi, Firenze.

Page 91 Ellen Quillan Collection, Institute of Texan Cultures.

Page 92 Frederick J. Pohl, *Amerigo Vespucci. . . .*

Page 94 Figures 1, 4 and 5 — Konrad Kretschmer, *Historia de. . . .* Figures 2 and 3 — R. y Gil Joaquin Diaz-Alejo, *America . . .,* number 117.

Page 95 *Harper's Weekly,* December 11, 1875, page 1008.

Page 96 Simon Grynæus, ed., *Novus Orbis . . .* (1555 edition), frontispiece.

Page 98 Konrad Kretschmer, *Historia de. . . .*

Page 99 M.B. Synge, *A Book of . . .,* page 207.

Page 100 M.B. Synge, *A Book of . . .,* page 213.

Running afoul of cannibals . . . a supposed common danger of New World explorers